Summary Guides

Maths 7

Dean Findlay

First published in 2024, reprinted in 2025, 2026.

Insight Publications Pty Ltd
3/350 Charman Road
Cheltenham Victoria 3192
Australia

Tel: +61 3 8571 4950
Email: books@insightpublications.com.au

www.insightpublications.com.au

Summary Guides – Maths 7 / Dean Findlay

ISBN: 9781923154544

Edited by Dr Geoffrey Marnell
Proofread by Owen Kavanagh and Olivia Shenken
Cover design by Melisa Paredes
Artwork by Artin Education
Typesetting by Aptara®, Inc.
Printed by Markono Print Media Pte Ltd

Insight Publications acknowledges the Traditional Custodians of the Country on which we meet and work, the Boonwurrung People of the Kulin Nation. We pay our respects to their Elders past and present, and extend that respect to all Aboriginal and Torres Strait Islander peoples.

Table of contents

Introduction

The *Summary Guides – Maths* series has been written by practising teachers who are passionate about creating user-friendly, accessible guides on mathematics.

The explanations and exercises in these guides develop core numeracy skills for personal, work and civic life, and provide the base knowledge for professional applications of maths as well as for mathematical specialisation. Maths is part of your daily life no matter what you choose to do as an adult – it is important for thinking critically and making sense of the world.

This book summarises key concepts in a clear and comprehensive way. It includes examples with worked solutions and step-by-step explanations, as well as exercises for you to complete. The best way to use this book is to make a habit of it, regularly working through the examples and exercises, and comparing your answers with those provided. Whether you commit to a daily, weekly or fortnightly routine, consistent practice is the key to your success.

Dean Findlay and Insight Publications

Dean Findlay holds tertiary qualifications in mathematics, education and applied learning. He has spent his teaching career empowering students to think mathematically and embrace problem-solving. Building on the work of varied educators and mathematicians, Dean aims to instil creativity and passion, while making mathematical concepts and processes accessible to all.

Chapter 1 – Numbers

Numbers are made up of the digits 0, 1, 2, 3, 4, 5, 6, 7, 8 and 9.

We use numbers every day for all types of mathematics.

1.1 Place value

The position of a digit in a number gives the digit its value. A **place value chart** can help you determine the value of each digit based on its position.

Here is an example of a place value chart for the number of people who attended the tennis on one day over the summer: 30 516.

Number	3	0	5	1	6
Place value	ten thousands	thousands	hundreds	tens	ones

Example

In the number 256, determine the place value of

a. the 2 **b.** the 5 **c.** the 6.

✓ *Solution*

Working	Explanation
a. hundreds	The 2 in the number 256 is in the hundreds place.
b. tens	The 5 in the number 256 is in the tens place.
c. ones	The 6 in the number 256 is in the ones place. **Note:** it is common to see the ones place called 'units'.

Exercise 1.1

For each number listed below, determine the place value of the digit in brackets.

a. 23 045 (2) **b.** 562 021 (6) **c.** 803 096 (8) **d.** 382 (8)

e. 538 (5) **f.** 36 (6) **g.** 4789 (7) **h.** 89 123 (9)

1.2 Number symbols

The following mathematical symbols are used to compare numbers.

Equal to	Not equal to	Greater than	Greater than or equal to	Less than	Less than or equal to
$=$	$\neq$	$>$	$\geq$	$<$	$\leq$

Example

Complete the following number sentences by placing the correct symbol in each box.

a. $317 \square 560$ **b.** $59 \square 56$ **c.** $56\,317 \square 56\,344$

✓ *Solution*

Working	Explanation
a. $317 \boxed{<} 560$	Reading from left to right we start by comparing the hundreds column. We see immediately that 300 is less than 500, so 317 is less than 560.
b. $59 \boxed{>} 56$	Reading from left to right we start by comparing the tens column. These columns are equal, so we move to the next column (the ones column). We see that 9 is greater than 6, so 59 is greater than 56.
c. $56\,317 \boxed{<} 56\,344$	Reading from left to right, the digits are equal until we reach the tens column. We see that 1 is less than 4, so 56 317 is less than 56 344.

Exercise 1.2.1

Complete the following number sentences by placing the correct symbol in each box.

a. $21 \square 25$ **b.** $234 \square 226$ **c.** $44\,557 \square 44\,516$

d. $87 \square 78$ **e.** $190\,381 \square 190\,234$ **f.** $879 \square 889$

Exercise 1.2.2

Complete the following number sentences by placing the correct symbol in each box.

a. $6 + 8 \square 40 \div 2$ **b.** $13 - 6 \square 12 + 5$ **c.** $4 + 3 + 2 \square 10$

d. $6 \times 8 \square 30 + 16$ **e.** $7 - 3 \square 18 \div 3$ **f.** $60 + 5 \square 7 \times 9$

1.3 Addition and subtraction of whole numbers

Addition and subtraction of whole numbers requires a good understanding of place value. Remember that **sum** means addition and **difference** means subtraction.

There are many ways to add and subtract in mathematics. In this summary guide we are going to explore two approaches: mental strategies, and addition and subtraction algorithms.

Mental strategies involve changing the numbers in a way that makes the calculation easy enough to be done in your head. An **algorithm** is a step-by-step process for deriving the answer to a problem.

Example

Calculate the following using **mental strategies**.

a. $37 + 38$ **b.** $54 + 22$ **c.** $126 + 125$

d. $94 - 49$ **e.** $88 - 43$ **f.** $100 - 42$

✓ ***Solution***

Working	Explanation
a. $37 + 38$ $40 + 40 = 80$ $80 - 5 = 75$	Round both numbers up to 40 and calculate the sum. $37(+3)$ and $38(+2)$ Then subtract the sum of the amounts we rounded both numbers up by: $3 + 2 = 5$.
b. $54 + 22$ $54 = 50 + 4$ and $22 = 20 + 2$	Separate 54 and 22 into their two place values.
$50 + 20 = 70$ $4 + 2 = 6$	Add the tens and ones separately.
$54 + 22 = 70 + 6 = 76$	Add the sum of the tens to the sum of the ones to get the final answer.
c. $125 + 1 + 125$ $125 \times 2 + 1 = 251$	Read 126 as $125 + 1$. Double 125 and then add 1.
d. $94 - 49 = 95 - 50$ $= 45$	Add 1 to both numbers. (The difference will be the same.) Now the subtraction will be easier.
e. $88 - 43$ $88 = 80 + 8$ and $43 = 40 + 3$	Separate 88 and 43 into their two place values.
$80 - 40 = 40$ $8 - 3 = 5$	Subtract the tens and ones separately.
$88 - 43 = 40 + 5 = 45$	Add the sum of the tens to the sum of the ones to get the final answer.
f. $100 - 42 = 100 - 40 - 2$ $= 58$	100 is easy to work with, so separate the 42 into tens and ones. Subtract all parts.

Example

Find the sum of 28 and 34 using the **addition algorithm**.

✓ ***Solution***

Working	Explanation
Step 1: $\begin{array}{r} 28 \\ +\ 34 \\ \hline \end{array}$	Set up the equation vertically with each digit lining up with its corresponding place value.
Step 2: $\begin{array}{r} {}^{1}28 \\ +\ 34 \\ \hline 2 \end{array}$	Starting from the right (the ones), add the digits together. Since the sum of 4 and 8 is greater than 9, write down the value of the ones and carry 1 over to the tens.
Step 3: $\begin{array}{r} {}^{1}28 \\ +\ 34 \\ \hline 62 \end{array}$	Add the digits in the tens column. Remember to add the 1 carried over from the previous step.

Example

Find the difference between 174 and 28 using the **subtraction algorithm.**

✓ Solution

Working	Explanation
Step 1: $\begin{array}{r} 174 \\ -\ \ 28 \\ \hline \end{array}$	Set up the equation vertically with each digit lining up with the corresponding place value.
Step 2. $\begin{array}{r} 1\overset{6}{\not7}\,{}^{1}4 \\ -\ \ 2\ 8 \\ \hline 6 \end{array}$	Starting from the right (the ones), subtract the bottom digit from the top digit. Since 8 is less than 4, we must borrow 1 from the tens column. We can then subtract 8 from 14.
Step 3: $\begin{array}{r} 1\overset{6}{\not7}\,{}^{1}4 \\ -\ \ 2\ 8 \\ \hline 1\ 4\ 6 \end{array}$	Subtract the digits in the tens column. Remember that the 7 tens are now 6 tens because we borrowed 1 ten in the previous step. Since there are no hundreds in the second line, carry the hundred from the first line down to the answer.

Exercise 1.3

Use an appropriate strategy to solve the following sum and difference problems.

a. $95 + 12$ **b.** $26 + 32$ **c.** $145 + 143$ **d.** $98 + 88$

e. $47 - 19$ **f.** $200 - 33$ **g.** $76 - 13$ **h.** $457 - 112$

1.4 Multiplication of whole numbers

As with addition and subtraction, there are many ways to multiply whole numbers. We will work through three common approaches to multiplying whole numbers.

Remember that sometimes the word **product** is used when we need to multiply numbers.

Example

Calculate the product of the following numbers where at least one number is a multiple of 10.

a. 42×10 **b.** 97×100 **c.** 20×80

✓ Solution

Working	Explanation
a. $42 \times 1\underline{0} = 420$	Multiplying any number by 10 just adds a zero to the end of the number.
b. $97 \times 1\underline{00} = 9700$	Multiplying any number by 100 just adds two zeros to the end of the number.

c. $20 \times 80 = 2 \times 10 \times 80$ $= 2 \times 800$ $= 1600$	Split either number into a product of 10 and complete the multiplication.

Example

Calculate the product of the following numbers using **mental strategies**.

a. 3×29 b. 25×12 c. 12×34

✓ Solution

Working	Explanation
a. $3 \times 29 = ?$ $3 \times 30 = 90$	Since 29 is close to 30, calculate the product of 3×30.
$90 - 3 = 87$	But we want 29 lots of 3 (not 30 lots of 3) so subtract one lot of 3 to get the final answer.
b. $25 \times 12 = ?$ $25 \times 2 = 50$ $12 \div 2 = 6$	Since 25 is an odd number and 12 is an even number, we can double the odd number and halve the even number. The product will be the same.
$50 \times 6 = 300$	Multiply the doubled number by the halved number to get the product.
c. $12 \times 34 = ?$ $10 + 2$	Split 12 into its place values: tens and ones.
$10 \times 34 = 340$ $2 \times 34 = 68$	Multiply each place value by 34.
$340 + 68 = 408$	Add both products together to get the final answer.

Example

Calculate the product of 46 and 5 using the **short multiplication algorithm**.

✓ Solution

Working	Explanation
$\begin{array}{r} {}^{3}46 \\ \times \quad 5 \\ \hline 0 \end{array}$	Set the numbers up vertically. Starting from the right, multiply the digits in the ones column. Since $6 \times 5 = 30$, carry the 3 over to the tens column.
$\begin{array}{r} {}^{3}46 \\ \times \quad 5 \\ \hline 230 \end{array}$	Multiply the 4 in the tens column by 5, and remember to add the 3 tens carried over from the previous step.

Example

Calculate the product of 246 and 15 using the **long multiplication algorithm**.

✓ Solution

Working	Explanation
$\begin{array}{r} {}^{2}2^{3}46 \\ \times \quad 15 \\ \hline 1230 \end{array}$	Set the numbers up vertically. Multiply 246 by 5 as we did in the previous example. Remember to add the numbers carried over to the tens and hundreds columns.
$\begin{array}{r} {}^{2}2^{3}46 \\ \times \quad 15 \\ \hline 1230 \\ +\ 2460 \\ \hline 3690 \end{array}$	Now multiply 246 by 10. Add the two products to get the final solution.

Exercise 1.4

Use an appropriate strategy to solve the following problems.

a. 36×3 **b.** 17×15 **c.** 21×8 **d.** 153×16

e. 8×18 **f.** 92×4 **g.** 84×23 **h.** 421×13

1.5 Division of whole numbers

Successful division relies upon a good knowledge of the multiplication tables.

Example

Evaluate each of the following.

a. $24 \div 6$ **b.** $96 \div 12$

✓ Solution

Working	Explanation
a. 4	From the multiplication tables we know that $6 \times 4 = 24$. Therefore $24 \div 6 = 4$.
b. 8	From the multiplication tables we know that $12 \times 8 = 96$. Therefore $96 \div 12 = 8$.

Example

Evaluate each of the following using short division.

a. $5\overline{)90}$ **b.** $6\overline{)612}$

✓ *Solution*

Working	Explanation
a. $\begin{array}{r} 1 \\ 5\overline{)9^{4}0} \end{array}$	Begin by asking 'how many fives go into 9?' Write the answer directly above the 9. There is a remainder of 4, so carry this over to the units column. The units column is now equivalent to 40.
$\begin{array}{r} 18 \\ 5\overline{)9^{4}0} \end{array}$	Now ask 'how many fives go into 40?' Write the answer directly above the 0.
b. $\begin{array}{r} 1 \\ 6\overline{)612} \end{array}$	Begin by asking 'how many sixes go into 6?' Write the answer directly above the 6.
$\begin{array}{r} 10 \\ 6\overline{)612} \end{array}$	Now 'how many sixes go into 1?' Write the answer, 0, directly above the 1.
$\begin{array}{r} 102 \\ 6\overline{)612} \end{array}$	To complete the division, ask 'how many sixes go into 12?' Write the answer directly above the 2.

✎ Exercise 1.5

Use an appropriate strategy to make the following calculations.

a. $120 \div 10$ **b.** $132 \div 12$ **c.** $450 \div 5$ **d.** $3456 \div 2$

e. $864 \div 16$ **f.** $1296 \div 27$ **g.** $468 \div 18$ **h.** $1083 \div 19$

1.6 Order of operations

The abbreviation **BIDMAS** can help you remember the correct order in which to perform mathematical operations.

Brackets	Indices	Division	Multiplication	Addition	Subtraction
()	x^n	$\div$	$\times$	$+$	$-$

Remember that when division and multiplication, or addition and subtraction, appear in the same calculation, you should always work from left to right.

Example

Simplify $4 \times 2 - (10 - 7)$.

✓ ***Solution***

Working	Explanation
$4 \times 2 - (10 - 7) = 4 \times 2 - 3$ $= 8 - 3$ $= 5$	Always evaluate an operation that is inside brackets first. Evaluate any multiplication or division before addition or subtraction. Evaluate any addition or subtraction.

Example

Simplify $10 \times 3 - 64 \div 8$.

✓ ***Solution***

Working	Explanation
$10 \times 3 - 64 \div 8 = 30 - 8$ $= 22$	Since both multiplication and division are in the problem, we must calculate from left to right, that is, multiplication first and then division. Then subtract 8 from 30 to get the final answer.

Example

Simplify $2^3 + (5 \times 3)$.

✓ ***Solution***

Working	Explanation
$2^3 + (5 \times 3) = 2^3 + 15$ $= 8 + 15$ $= 23$	Evaluate operations inside brackets first. Indices next: $2^3 = 2 \times 2 \times 2 = 8$ Finally add 8 and 15 to get the answer.

Exercise 1.6

Simplify the following.

a. $8 + 3 \times 10$
b. $8 \times 5 - 4 \times 10$
c. $(28 + 10) \div 2$
d. $88 \div 8 - (3 \times 2)$
e. $12 \times 5 \times (10 - 4)$
f. $2^2 + (3 + 6) \times 6$
g. $4^2 \div 8 \times 10$
h. $13 - 4 + 5 \times 4$

1.7 Estimation

Estimation is an important concept in mathematics. It is a way of checking whether our answers are reasonable.

Estimating is not the same as guessing, because when we estimate we base it on the information given in the question.

To estimate effectively, we need to be able to round whole numbers.

Example

Round 52 to the nearest 10.

✓ ***Solution***

Working	Explanation
$5\underline{2}$ Round down to 50.	When rounding to the nearest 10, we look at the digit in the ones column. Since it is less than 5 we round down, that is, to 50. Another way of thinking about the question is to ask, 'is 52 closer to 50 or 60?'

Example

Round 231 to the leading digit.

✓ ***Solution***

Working	Explanation
$2\underline{3}1$ Round down to 200.	Rounding to the leading digit in this case means rounding to the nearest 100. Look at the digit in the tens column. Since it is less than 5 we round down, that is, to 200. You could ask, 'is 231 closer to 200 or 300?'

Example

Estimate the answer to 106×94 by rounding both numbers to the nearest 100.

✓ ***Solution***

Working	Explanation
$100 \times 100 = 10\,000$ Therefore $106 \times 94 \approx 10\,000$.	Round both 106 and 94 to 100 and multiply.

Example

Estimate the answer to $3457 \div 9$ by rounding both numbers to the nearest 10.

✓ Solution

Working	Explanation
$3460 \div 10 = 346$	3457 rounded to the nearest 10 is 3460.
Therefore $3457 \div 9 \approx 346$.	9 rounded to the nearest 10 is 10.
	Divide, but using both rounded numbers.

Example

Estimate the answer to 51×6 by rounding both numbers to the leading digit.

✓ Solution

Working	Explanation
$50 \times 6 = 300$	51 rounds to 50.
Therefore $51 \times 6 \approx 300$.	6 cannot be rounded. Multiply it by 50.

Exercise 1.7

Round the following to the leading digits to estimate the solutions.

a. 681×41 **b.** 104×8946 **c.** 950×3489 **d.** 141×837

e. $2840 \div 41$ **f.** $3599 \div 52$ **g.** $1955 \div 48$ **h.** $44\,895 \div 15$

Answers

Exercise 1.1

a. ten thousands b. ten thousands c. hundred thousands

d. tens e. hundreds f. ones

g. hundreds h. thousands

Exercise 1.2.1

a. $21 \boxed{<} 25$ b. $234 \boxed{>} 226$ c. $44\,557 \boxed{>} 44\,516$

d. $87 \boxed{>} 78$ e. $190\,381 \boxed{>} 190\,234$ f. $879 \boxed{<} 889$

Exercise 1.2.2

a. $6 + 8 \boxed{<} 40 \div 2$ b. $13 - 6 \boxed{<} 12 + 5$ c. $4 + 3 + 2 \boxed{<} 10$

d. $6 \times 8 \boxed{>} 30 + 16$ e. $7 - 3 \boxed{<} 18 \div 3$ f. $60 + 5 \boxed{>} 7 \times 9$

Exercise 1.3

a. 107	b. 58	c. 288	d. 186
e. 28	f. 167	g. 63	h. 345

Exercise 1.4

a. 108	b. 255	c. 168	d. 2448
e. 144	f. 368	g. 1932	h. 5473

Exercise 1.5

a. 12	b. 11	c. 90	d. 1728
e. 54	f. 48	g. 26	h. 57

Exercise 1.6

a. 38	b. 0	c. 19	d. 5
e. 360	f. 58	g. 20	h. 29

Exercise 1.7

a. 28 000	b. 900 000	c. 3 000 000	d. 80 000
e. 75	f. 80	g. 40	h. 2000

Chapter 2 – Fractions

Fractions are a mathematical way of showing parts of a whole number.

The top number is the **numerator** and the bottom number is the **denominator**.

numerator ⟶ $\frac{3}{4}$ ⟵ denominator

2.1 Types of fractions

A **proper** fraction has a smaller numerator than the denominator, for example $\frac{2}{11}$.

An **improper** fraction has a larger numerator than the denominator, for example, $\frac{9}{4}$.

An improper fraction can be converted into a whole number with a fraction. We call this a **mixed number.** For example, $\frac{9}{4} = 2\frac{1}{4}$.

Example

Consider the following diagram.

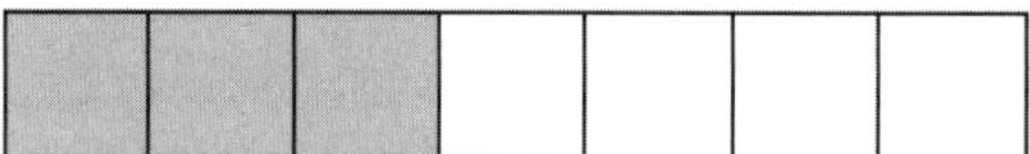

a. Write a proper fraction in the form of $\frac{\text{shaded squares}}{\text{total squares}}$

b. Write a proper fraction in the form of $\frac{\text{unshaded squares}}{\text{total squares}}$

✓ *Solution*

Working	Explanation
a. $\frac{3}{7}$	There are 3 shaded squares out of a total of 7 squares.
b. $\frac{4}{7}$	There are 4 unshaded squares out of a total of 7 squares.

Example

Consider the following diagram.

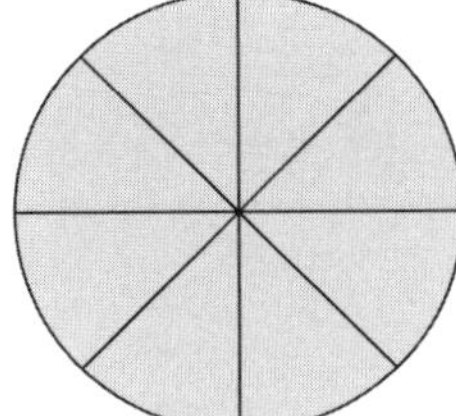 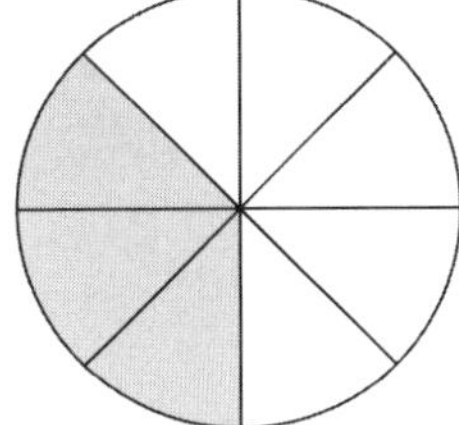

a. How many shaded sectors are pictured in both circles?

b. Write a mixed number that represents the shaded sectors of both circles.

c. Convert the mixed number from part **b.** into an improper fraction.

✓ Solution

Working	Explanation
a. 11 shaded sectors in total	Each circle is divided equally into 8 sectors. Eight sectors are shaded in the first circle and 3 are shaded in the second circle, making 11 in total.
b. $1\frac{3}{8}$	Eight out of 8 sectors are shaded in the first circle $\left(\frac{8}{8}=1\right)$ and 3 out of 8 sectors are shaded in the second circle $\left(\frac{3}{8}\right)$. Write both together to form a mixed number.
c. $\frac{11}{8}$	Multiply the whole number by the denominator: $1 \times 8 = 8$. Add the numerators: $8 + 3 + 11$. The improper fraction is the number you have just calculated over the same denominator.

Exercise 2.1.1

Consider the following diagram.

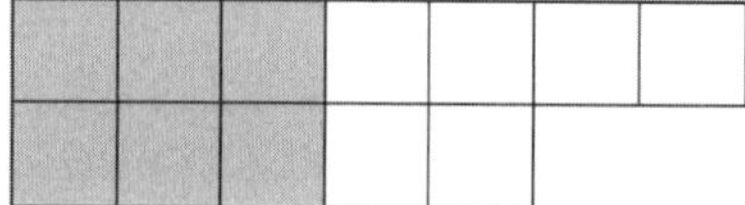

a. How many total squares are pictured?

b. Write a proper fraction that shows

   i. the number of shaded squares out of the total number of squares

   ii. the number of unshaded squares out of the total number of squares.

Exercise 2.1.2

Consider the following diagram.

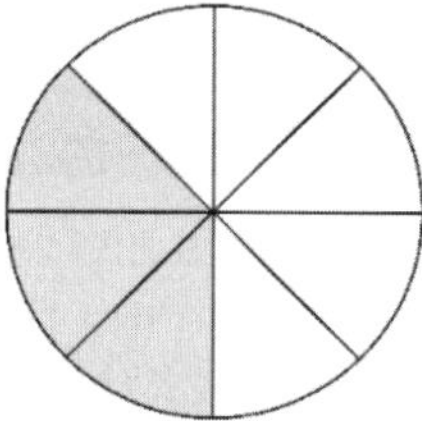

a. How many sectors is the circle divided into?

b. Write a proper fraction that shows

   i. the number of shaded sectors out of the total number of sectors

   ii. the number of unshaded sectors out of the total number of sectors.

2.2 Equivalent fractions

When two fractions have the same ratio, they are **equivalent**. For example, $\frac{1}{2}$ is equivalent to $\frac{3}{6}$, as the numerators are in the same ratio $(1 \text{ to } 3)$ as the denominators.

Equivalent fractions will be on the same spot on a number line.

If two fractions are equivalent, we can say that they are equal $(=)$.

Example

Consider the two shapes pictured below.

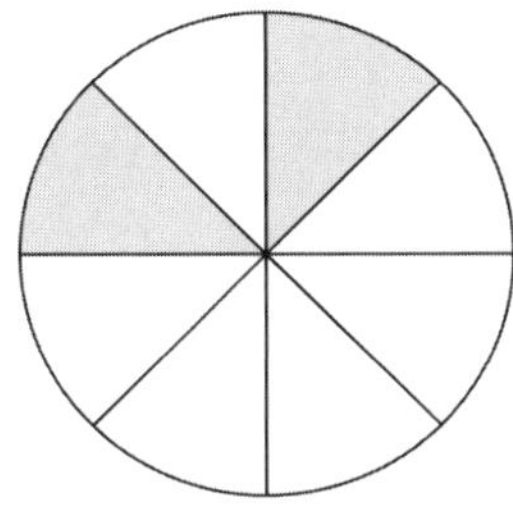

Shape 1

Shape 2

a. Write a proper fraction for the shaded sectors in Shape 1.

b. Write a proper fraction for the shaded square in Shape 2.

c. Mark both fractions on a number line to show they are equivalent.

✓ Solution

Working	Explanation
a. $\frac{2}{8}$	There are 2 shaded sectors out of a total of 8 sectors.
b. $\frac{1}{4}$	There is 1 shaded square out of a total of 4 squares.
c. Number lines: 0, $\frac{1}{4}$, $\frac{2}{4}$, $\frac{3}{4}$, 1 (dot at $\frac{1}{4}$) 0, $\frac{2}{8}$, $\frac{4}{8}$, $\frac{6}{8}$, 1 (dot at $\frac{2}{8}$)	Draw one number line above another number line with the whole numbers aligned. On the top number line divide the whole numbers into four equally spaced intervals. Place a dot at the first interval after 0, representing the number $\frac{1}{4}$. On the bottom number line divide the whole numbers into eight equally spaced intervals. Place a dot at the second interval after 0, representing the number $\frac{2}{8}$. You will find that both dots are perfectly aligned.

Exercise 2.2

Complete each of the following number sentences by writing >, < or = in the empty box.

a. $\frac{5}{9}\square\frac{2}{5}$ b. $\frac{3}{5}\square\frac{6}{10}$ c. $\frac{2}{3}\square\frac{3}{5}$ d. $\frac{7}{8}\square\frac{3}{4}$

e. $\frac{3}{8}\square\frac{6}{16}$ f. $\frac{8}{9}\square\frac{9}{10}$ g. $\frac{1}{3}\square\frac{1}{2}$ h. $\frac{2}{9}\square\frac{11}{36}$

2.3 Simplifying fractions

A fraction can be written in its **simplest form** if both the numerator and denominator can be divided by a common factor.

Example

Write $\frac{16}{20}$ in its simplest form.

✓ Solution

Working	Explanation
$\frac{16}{20}=\frac{4\times 4}{4\times 5}$ $=\frac{\cancel{4}\times 4}{\cancel{4}\times 5}$ $=\frac{4}{5}$	To simplify a fraction we look for the highest common factor of both the numerator and denominator. In this example, 4 is the highest factor of 16 and 20. We can now express the original fraction as a simpler fraction multiplied by $\frac{4}{4}$. Since $\frac{4}{4}=1$ we can cancel it, leaving just the simplified fraction.

Example

Write $\frac{9}{36}$ in its simplest form.

✓ Solution

Working	Explanation
$\frac{9}{36}=\frac{9\times 1}{9\times 4}$ $=\frac{\cancel{9}\times 1}{\cancel{9}\times 4}$ $=\frac{1}{4}$	In this example, 9 is the highest common factor of 9 and 36: 1, 3, $\boxed{9}$ 1, 2, 3, 4, 6, $\boxed{9}$, 12, 18, 36 We can now express the original fraction as a simpler fraction multiplied by $\frac{9}{9}$. Since $\frac{9}{9}=1$ we can cancel it, leaving just the simplified fraction.

Exercise 2.3

Simplify the following fractions.

a. $\frac{8}{64}$ b. $\frac{16}{28}$ c. $\frac{30}{42}$ d. $\frac{24}{32}$

e. $\frac{15}{20}$ f. $\frac{9}{54}$ g. $\frac{40}{90}$ h. $\frac{27}{81}$

2.4 Addition and subtraction of fractions

Fractions can only be added or subtracted if they share a **common denominator**.

We prefer to leave answers as improper fractions unless we are told to do otherwise.

Example

Evaluate $\frac{1}{5}+\frac{1}{2}$.

✓ Solution

Working	Explanation
$\frac{1}{5}+\frac{1}{2}=\frac{2}{10}+\frac{5}{10}$ $=\frac{7}{10}$	To add two fractions, we must first find the lowest common denominator. Write down the multiples of each denominator and look for the first multiple that is common to both denominators. This will be the lowest common multiple. $2, 4, 6, 8, \boxed{10}, 12, \ldots$ $5, \boxed{10}, 15, \ldots$ We can see that 10 is the lowest common denominator of $\frac{1}{5}$ and $\frac{1}{2}$. Taking each fraction in turn, convert it to an equivalent fraction with the denominator equal to the lowest common multiple. Another way of thinking about this is to multiply both the numerator and denominator by the number that will make the denominator equal to the lowest common multiple (10). Multiplying $\frac{1}{5}$ by $\frac{2}{2}$ will give an equivalent fraction with a denominator of 10, and multiplying $\frac{1}{2}$ by $\frac{5}{5}$ will give an equivalent fraction with a denominator of 10. Now that we have equivalent fractions with the same denominator, we can add the numerators.

Example

Evaluate $\frac{3}{4} - \frac{7}{10}$.

✓ ***Solution***

Working	Explanation
$\frac{3}{4} - \frac{7}{10} = \frac{15}{20} - \frac{14}{20}$ $= \frac{1}{20}$	Find the first common multiple of the denominators: $4, 8, 12, 16, \boxed{20}, 24, \ldots$ $10, \boxed{20}, 30, \ldots$ 20 is the lowest common denominator of $\frac{3}{4}$ and $\frac{7}{10}$. Convert each fraction to an equivalent fraction with a denominator of 20 (that is, multiply the first numerator by 5 and the second numerator by 2). Now that we have equivalent fractions with the same denominator, we can subtract the numerators.

Example

Evaluate $1 + \frac{2}{5}$.

✓ ***Solution***

Working	Explanation
$1 + \frac{2}{5} = \frac{5}{5} + \frac{2}{5}$ $= \frac{7}{5}$	Convert the whole number into a fraction that has the same denominator as the fraction being added: $1 = \frac{1}{1} = \frac{5}{5}$ Once both fractions have the same denominator, we can add the numerators.

Example

Evaluate $2 - \frac{3}{8}$.

✓ ***Solution***

Working	Explanation
$2 - \frac{3}{8} = \frac{16}{8} - \frac{3}{8}$ $= \frac{13}{8}$	Convert the whole number into a fraction that has the same denominator as the fraction being subtracted: $2 = \frac{2}{1} = \frac{16}{8}$ Once both fractions have the same denominator, we can subtract the numerators.

Exercise 2.4

Evaluate the following, giving the final answer in its simplest form.

a. $\frac{3}{10}+\frac{1}{10}$ b. $\frac{4}{55}+\frac{2}{11}$ c. $\frac{2}{3}-\frac{2}{9}$ d. $\frac{7}{10}-\frac{1}{4}$

e. $\frac{17}{30}+\frac{5}{6}$ f. $\frac{7}{12}+1$ g. $2-\frac{7}{20}$ h. $\frac{2}{3}-\frac{7}{22}$

2.5 Multiplication of fractions

When multiplying a number by a proper fraction, the resulting product will be smaller than the original number.

Example

Evaluate $\frac{2}{5}\times\frac{3}{7}$.

✓ Solution

Working	Explanation
$\frac{2}{5}\times\frac{3}{7}=\frac{2\times 3}{5\times 7}$ $=\frac{6}{35}$	Multiply the numerators and denominators separately. Think of the numerators and denominators as requiring individual operations.

Example

Evaluate $\frac{5}{8}\times\frac{3}{20}$.

✓ Solution

Working	Explanation
$\frac{5}{8}\times\frac{3}{20}=\frac{{}^{1}\cancel{5}}{8}\times\frac{3}{\cancel{20}_{4}}$ $=\frac{1\times 3}{8\times 4}$ $=\frac{3}{32}$	Before multiplying the numerators and denominators, look to see if any simplifying is possible. Simplifying before multiplying will result in the final product being in its simplest form.

Example

Evaluate $3 \times \frac{2}{5}$.

✓ ***Solution***

Working	Explanation
$3 \times \frac{2}{5} = \frac{3}{1} \times \frac{2}{5}$ $= \frac{3 \times 2}{1 \times 5}$ $= \frac{6}{5}$	Convert the whole number into a fraction: $3 = \frac{3}{1}$ Multiply the numerators and denominators separately.

Example

Evaluate $4 \times \frac{5}{12}$.

✓ ***Solution***

Working	Explanation
$4 \times \frac{5}{12} = \frac{4}{1} \times \frac{5}{12}$ $= \frac{{}^{1}\not{4}}{1} \times \frac{5}{\not{12}_{3}}$ $= \frac{5}{3}$	Convert the whole number into a fraction: $4 = \frac{4}{1}$ Look for any simplification. Multiply the numerators and denominators separately.

Exercise 2.5

Evaluate the following, giving the final answer in its simplest form.

a. $\frac{4}{5} \times \frac{5}{9}$ b. $\frac{2}{9} \times \frac{15}{16}$ c. $\frac{5}{2} \times \frac{2}{15}$ d. $\frac{25}{6} \times \frac{12}{5}$

e. $3 \times \frac{2}{9}$ f. $\frac{3}{4} \times 8$ g. $\frac{5}{8} \times 2$ h. $3 \times \frac{5}{12}$

2.6 Division of fractions

To divide by a fraction, multiply the fraction being divided by the **reciprocal** of the fraction that you want to divide by. The reciprocal of a fraction is where the numerator and denominator are flipped; that is, the numerator becomes the denominator and the denominator becomes the numerator.

We prefer to leave answers as improper fractions unless we are told to do otherwise.

Example

Evaluate $\frac{3}{4} \div \frac{2}{5}$.

✓ ***Solution***

Working	Explanation
$\frac{3}{4} \div \frac{2}{5} = \frac{3}{4} \times \frac{5}{2}$ $= \frac{15}{8}$	**Keep** the first fraction the same. **Change** the division to multiplication. **Flip** the second fraction (so that it becomes its reciprocal). **Multiply** the first fraction and the reciprocal of the second fraction.

Example

Evaluate $12 \div \frac{1}{2}$.

✓ ***Solution***

Working	Explanation
$12 \div \frac{1}{2} = \frac{12}{1} \times \frac{2}{1}$ $= 24$	Change the whole number into a fraction. Keep, change and flip (as before). Multiply the fractions together. In this example the answer is easy to understand, as there are 24 halves in 12 wholes.

Example

Evaluate $\frac{1}{4} \div 3$.

✓ ***Solution***

Working	Explanation
$\frac{1}{4} \div 3 = \frac{1}{4} \div \frac{3}{1}$ $= \frac{1}{4} \times \frac{1}{3}$ $= \frac{1}{12}$	Change the whole number into a fraction. Keep, change and flip. Multiply the fractions together.

Exercise 2.6

Evaluate the following, giving the final answer in its simplest form.

a. $\frac{4}{5} \div \frac{4}{9}$ b. $\frac{5}{8} \div \frac{25}{12}$ c. $\frac{16}{5} \div \frac{32}{15}$ d. $\frac{14}{9} \div \frac{49}{18}$

e. $5 \div \frac{3}{7}$ f. $6 \div \frac{2}{3}$ g. $3 \div \frac{5}{6}$ h. $2 \div \frac{1}{2}$

Answers

Exercise 2.1.1

a. 12 b. i. $\frac{6}{12} = \frac{1}{2}$ ii. $\frac{6}{12} = \frac{1}{2}$

Exercise 2.1.2

a. 8 b. i. $\frac{3}{8}$ ii. $\frac{5}{8}$

Exercise 2.2

a. $\frac{5}{9} \boxed{>} \frac{2}{5}$ b. $\frac{3}{5} \boxed{=} \frac{6}{10}$ c. $\frac{2}{3} \boxed{>} \frac{3}{5}$ d. $\frac{7}{8} \boxed{>} \frac{3}{4}$

e. $\frac{3}{8} \boxed{=} \frac{6}{16}$ f. $\frac{8}{9} \boxed{<} \frac{9}{10}$ g. $\frac{1}{3} \boxed{<} \frac{1}{2}$ h. $\frac{2}{9} \boxed{<} \frac{11}{36}$

Exercise 2.3

a. $\frac{1}{8}$ b. $\frac{4}{7}$ c. $\frac{5}{7}$ d. $\frac{3}{4}$

e. $\frac{3}{4}$ f. $\frac{1}{6}$ g. $\frac{4}{9}$ h. $\frac{1}{3}$

Exercise 2.4

a. $\frac{2}{5}$ b. $\frac{14}{55}$ c. $\frac{4}{9}$ d. $\frac{9}{20}$

e. $\frac{7}{5}$ f. $\frac{19}{12}$ g. $\frac{33}{20}$ h. $\frac{23}{66}$

Exercise 2.5

a. $\frac{4}{9}$ b. $\frac{5}{24}$ c. $\frac{1}{3}$ d. 10

e. $\frac{2}{3}$ f. 6 g. $\frac{5}{4}$ h. $\frac{5}{4}$

Exercise 2.6

a. $\frac{9}{5}$ b. $\frac{3}{10}$ c. $\frac{3}{2}$ d. $\frac{4}{7}$

e. $\frac{35}{3}$ f. 9 g. $\frac{18}{5}$ h. 4

Chapter 3 – Decimals

Decimals appear widely in the world around us. Money, weights, lengths and world records are all expressed using decimals.

In this chapter we explore some of the skills needed to understand and calculate with decimals.

3.1 Place value of decimals

Just as there is a **place value** for each digit in an integer, there is a place value for each digit in a decimal. The diagram below shows the place value of each digit in the number 936.4156.

Hundreds	Tens	Ones	Decimal point	Tenths	Hundredths	Thousandths	Ten-thousandths
9	3	6	.	4	1	5	6

Example

In the each of the following numbers, determine the place value of the digit 3.

a. 64.31 **b.** 2.03 **c.** 0.00312 **d.** 1.31

✓ Solution

Working	Explanation
a. tenths	The 3 in the number 64.31 is in the **first** position to the right of the decimal point.
b. hundredths	The 3 in the number 2.03 is in the **second** position to the right of the decimal point.
c. thousandths	The 3 in the number 0.00312 is in the **third** position to the right of the decimal point.
d. tenths	The 3 in the number 1.31 is in the **first** position to the right of the decimal point.

Exercise 3.1

Write the value of the 7 in each of the following numbers in words.

a. 5.734	**b.** 0.0076	**c.** 1.27	**d.** 8.1307
e. 0.0078	**f.** 0.75	**g.** 103.07	**h.** 9.3557

3.2 Comparing decimals

Knowing the place value of the digits in decimals can help us to decide whether one decimal is larger than or smaller than another decimal. Another way to compare decimals is to plot them on a number line.

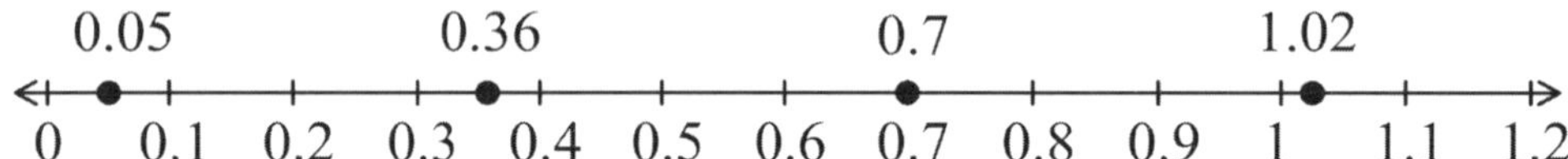

The number line above is in **ascending** order (that is, it goes from smallest to largest) from left to right, so the four decimals shown above the line (0.05, 0.36, 0.7 and 1.02) also go from smallest to largest.

We can use the greater than sign (>), less than sign (<) or equals sign (=) to compare decimals without using a number line.

Example

Complete the number sentence 2.3 ☐ 2.03 by writing the correct symbol (<, > or =) in the empty box.

✓ ***Solution***

Working	Explanation
2.3 [>] 2.03	The units are the same value (2), so ignore these digits and compare the tenths. Three tenths is larger than zero tenths. Therefore 2.3 is greater than 2.03.

Example

Complete the number sentence 0.51 ☐ 0.64 by writing the correct symbol (<, > or =) in the empty box.

✓ ***Solution***

Working	Explanation
$0.51 \boxed{<} 0.64$	The units are the same value (0), so ignore these digits and compare the tenths. Five tenths is smaller than six tenths. Therefore 0.51 is less than 0.64.

Example

Complete the number sentence $5.7 \square 5.70$ by writing the correct symbol ($<$, $>$ or $=$) in the empty box.

✓ ***Solution***

Working	Explanation
$5.7 \boxed{=} 5.70$	The units are the same value (5), so ignore these digits and compare the tenths. The tenths are the same value (7), so ignore these digits and compare the hundredths. The hundredths are the same value (0). Therefore 5.7 is equal to 5.70. **Note:** you do not need to continue writing zeros after a decimal number has terminated.

Exercise 3.2

Write $<$, $>$ or $=$ in the empty box between each of the following pairs of decimals to make the number sentence correct.

a. $0.65 \square 0.57$ **b.** $2.4 \square 0.42$ **c.** $0.303 \square 0.333$

d. $2.32 \square 1.955$ **e.** $4.70 \square 4.7$ **f.** $0.08 \square 0.80$

3.3 Rounding decimals

As with rounding any number, we need to think about how many digits we are keeping and then look at the *next* digit before deciding whether to round up or round down. If the next digit is 5 or greater, we round up. If it is less than 5, we round down.

We can also think about rounding as asking 'which number are we closer to?'

Example

Round 2.85 to one decimal place.

✓ ***Solution***

Working	Explanation
2.9	We are keeping one decimal (the tenth), so look at the next digit to the right of the tenth (the hundredth). It is 5. Therefore, we round up: the 8 becomes 9.

Example

Round 3.4619 to two decimal places.

✓ ***Solution***

Working	Explanation
3.46	We are keeping two decimals (the tenth and the hundredth), so look at the next digit to the right of the hundredth (the thousandth). It is 1, which is less than 5. This means that we round down: the 6 does not change and we remove all the decimals after it. Think: is 61 closer to 60 or 70?

Example

Round 12.0908 to three decimal places.

✓ ***Solution***

Working	Explanation
12.091	We are keeping three decimals (the tenth, hundredth and thousandth), so look at the next digit to the right of the thousandth (the ten-thousandth). It is 8, which is greater than 5. So we round up by changing the 0 to 1. Think: is 908 closer to 900 or 910?

Example

Round 9.98 to the nearest whole number.

✓ ***Solution***

Working	Explanation
10	We are not keeping any decimals (only units), so look at the next digit to the right of the unit (the tenth). It is 9, which is greater than 5. Therefore, we round up: from 9 to 10. Think: is 9.98 closer to 9 or 10?

Exercise 3.3

Round each of the following decimals to the number of decimal places shown in brackets.

a. 4.88 (1) **b.** 6.72 (1) **c.** 7.635 (2) **d.** 4.552 (2)

e. 0.6416 (3) **f.** 6.3637 (2) **g.** 4.333 (1) **h.** 0.7071 (3)

3.4 Addition and subtraction of decimals

As with adding and subtracting integers, we need to place our numbers into columns of the same place value before we add or subtract. Let's see how we do this with the simple calculation 1.06 + 9.3.

Step 1. Place the numbers so that the decimal points are vertically aligned (that is, one is directly above the other).	$\begin{array}{r} 1.06 \\ +\ 9.3 \\ \hline \end{array}$
Step 2. Add a 0 after the 9.3 so that both numbers have the same number of decimal places. (We can do this because 9.3 and 9.30 are the same number.)	$\begin{array}{r} 1.06 \\ +\ 9.30 \\ \hline \end{array}$
Step 3. Add the values as we do with whole numbers (starting from the right). Make sure that the decimal point in the final answer is in the same position as the decimal points above it.	$\begin{array}{r} 1.06 \\ +\ 9.30 \\ \hline 10.36 \end{array}$

Example

Calculate $3.55 + 6.83$.

✓ ***Solution***

Working	Explanation
$\begin{array}{r} 3.55 \\ +\ 6.83 \\ \hline 10.38 \end{array}$	Both 3.55 and 6.83 have the same number of decimal places. Line up both decimal points vertically and add the numbers from right to left. Make sure that the final answer has a decimal point in the same position.

Example

Calculate $11.83 - 10.04$.

✓ ***Solution***

Working	Explanation
$\begin{array}{r} 11.83 \\ -\ 10.04 \\ \hline 1.79 \end{array}$	Both 11.83 and 10.04 have the same number of decimal places. Line up both decimal points vertically and subtract from right to left as we do with whole numbers. Remember to borrow if needed. Make sure that the final answer has a decimal point in the same position.

Example

Calculate $7.21 + 0.003 + 1.139$.

✓ ***Solution***

Working	Explanation
$\begin{array}{r} 7.210 \\ 0.003 \\ +\ 1.139 \\ \hline 8.352 \end{array}$	Write 7.21 as 7.210 so that it has the same number of decimal places as the other numbers. Line up all decimal points vertically and add all numbers from right to left. Make sure that the final answer has a decimal point in the same position.

Example

Calculate $20 - 1.83$.

✓ Solution

Working	Explanation
$\begin{array}{r} 20.00 \\ -\ 1.83 \\ \hline 18.17 \end{array}$	Write 20 as 20.00 so that it has the same number of decimal places as the other number. Line up both decimal points vertically and subtract from right to left like we do with whole numbers. Remember to borrow if needed. Make sure that the final answer has a decimal point in the same position.

Exercise 3.4.1

Calculate the following expressions.

a. $3.76 + 5.22$ **b.** $9.2 + 8.8$ **c.** $7.21 + 0.6$ **d.** $2.314 + 4.21$

Exercise 3.4.2

Calculate the following expressions.

a. $8.45 - 6.21$ **b.** $7.63 - 4.14$ **c.** $3.5 - 0.87$ **d.** $10 - 6.69$

3.5 Multiplying decimals by multiples of ten

When multiplying a decimal by 10, 100, 1000 or another power of 10, we can quickly find the answer just by moving the decimal point to the right.

Example

Calculate 2.31×1000.

✓ Solution

Working	Explanation
$2.31 \times 1\underline{000} = 2.310 \times 1\underline{000}$ $= 2310$	The multiplier has 3 zeros, so we move the decimal point 3 places to the right. It may be easier to add some zeros on the end of 2.31 before moving the decimal point. If the final answer does not contain decimals, the decimal point does not need to be included, as the answer is a whole number.

Example

Calculate 0.0443×100.

✓ *Solution*

Working	Explanation
$0.0443 \times 1\underline{00} = 004.43$ $= 4.43$	The multiplier has 2 zeros, so we move the decimal point 2 places to the right. Write the final answer in a logical way (that is, without any zeros before the actual number).

Example

Calculate 83.42×10.

✓ *Solution*

Working	Explanation
$83.42 \times 1\underline{0} = 834.2$	The multiplier has 1 zero, so we move the decimal point 1 place to the right.

Example

Calculate $3.508 \times 10\ 000$.

✓ *Solution*

Working	Explanation
$3.508 \times 1\underline{0}\ \underline{000} = 3.5080 \times 1\underline{0}\ \underline{000}$ $= 35\ 080$ $= 35\ 080$	The multiplier has 4 zeros, so we move the decimal point 4 places to the right. It may be easier to add some zeros on the end of 3.508 before moving the decimal point. If the final answer does not contain decimals, the decimal point does not need to be included, as the answer is a whole number.

There are two main approaches to multiplying a decimal by a multiple of 10 that is not a power of 10 (that is, not 10, 100, 1000 and so on). In both cases we convert the multiple of 10 to a power of 10 multiplied by another number. For example, 5000 is converted to 1000×5. We then multiply the other number by both of the converted numbers. The two approaches differ only in the order in which we carry out the final multiplications.

Example

Calculate 3.52×2000.

✓ ***Solution***

Working	Explanation
$3.52 \times 2000 = 3.52 \times 2 \times 1\underline{000}$ $= 7.04 \times 1\underline{000}$ $= 7040$	Think of 2000 as 2×1000. Now consider whether it is easier to multiply by 2 first or 1000 first. In this example it is easier to multiply by 2: $3.52 \times 2 = 7.04$. Finally, multiply by 1000 by moving the decimal point 3 places to the right.

Example

Calculate 0.523×7000.

✓ ***Solution***

Working	Explanation
$0.523 \times 7000 = 0.523 \times 1\underline{000} \times 7$ $= 523 \times 7$ $= 3661$	Think of 7000 as 1000×7. Now consider whether it is easier to multiply by 7 first or 1000 first. In this example it is easier to multiply by 1000 first, so move the decimal point 3 places to the right. Finally, multiply 523 by 7.

Exercise 3.5.1

Calculate the following expressions.

a. 8.24×100 **b.** 7.112×10 **c.** $0.351 \times 10\,000$ **d.** 2.1×1000

Exercise 3.5.2

Calculate the following expressions.

a. 8.54×50 **b.** 2.21×3000 **c.** 5.002×6000 **d.** 0.87×500

3.6 Multiplying decimals by decimals

When multiplying numbers with decimals in them, the number of decimal places in the answer must equal the number of decimal places in the question.

Example

Calculate 5.5×0.4.

✓ ***Solution***

Working	Explanation
$\begin{array}{r} 55 \\ \times \quad 4 \\ \hline 220 \end{array}$	Ignore the decimal points and calculate 55×4.
There are 2 decimal places in total.	Add the number of decimal places in both numbers being multiplied. $5.\underline{5} \times 0.\underline{4}$ There is a total of 2 decimal places, so this must be the number of decimal places in the answer.
$5.5 \times 0.4 = 2.20$	Place a decimal point in the answer 2 places from the right.

Example

Calculate 20.3×0.05.

✓ ***Solution***

Working	Explanation
$\begin{array}{r} 203 \\ \times \quad 5 \\ \hline 1015 \end{array}$	Ignore the decimal points and calculate 203×5.
There are 3 decimal places in total.	Add the number of decimal places in both numbers being multiplied. $20.\underline{3} \times 0.\underline{05}$ There is a total of 3 decimal places, so this must be the number of decimal places in the answer.
$20.3 \times 0.05 = 1.015$	Place a decimal point in the answer 3 places from the right.

Exercise 3.6

Calculate the following expressions.

a. 0.9×0.2	**b.** 0.6×0.12	**c.** 0.14×0.5	**d.** 0.15×0.11
e. 3.2×0.4	**f.** 5.1×0.2	**g.** 6.2×4.1	**h.** 0.02×42

3.7 Division with decimals

When dividing a decimal by a whole number, we set up the division as usual, and keep the same number of decimal points in the answer as there is in the question.

Example

Calculate $39.6 \div 3$.

✓ Solution

Working	Explanation
$3\overline{)39.6}$	Set up short division as we do when dividing whole numbers.
$\begin{array}{r} 13.2 \\ 3\overline{)39.6} \end{array}$	Complete the short division by asking: • how many 3s go into 3 • how many 3s go into 9 and • how many 3s go into 6? Since 3 goes evenly into 39.6 the decimal terminates. Keep the decimal points in line.

Example

Calculate $18.4 \div 5$.

✓ Solution

Working	Explanation
$5\overline{)18.4}$	Set up short division as we do when dividing whole numbers.
$\begin{array}{r} 3. \\ 5\overline{)18.{}^{3}4} \end{array}$	Begin the short division by asking how many fives go into 18. Write the answer (3) followed by a decimal point.
$\begin{array}{r} 3.\,6 \\ 5\overline{)18.{}^{3}4{}^{4}0} \end{array}$	Since there is a remainder of 3, the 4 tenths become 34 tenths. We now ask how many fives go into 34. Since there is a remainder of 4, the 4 hundredths become 40 hundredths. We now ask how many fives go into 40.
$\begin{array}{r} 3.\,6\,8 \\ 5\overline{)18.{}^{3}4{}^{4}0} \end{array}$	Since there are exactly 8 fives in 40, the decimal terminates.

When dividing a decimal by a whole number multiple of 10 we apply the same techniques as when multiplying, but the decimal point will move to the left rather than the right.

Example

Calculate $881.6 \div 10$.

✓ Solution

Working	Explanation
$881.6 \div 1\underline{0} = 88.16$	The divisor has 1 zero, so we move the decimal point 1 place to the left.

Example

Calculate $881.6 \div 100$.

✓ Solution

Working	Explanation
$881.6 \div 1\underline{00} = 8.816$	The divisor has 2 zeros, so we move the decimal point 2 places to the left.

Example

Calculate $881.6 \div 200$.

✓ ***Solution***

Working	Explanation
$881.6 \div 2\underline{00} = 881.6 \div 1\underline{00} \div 2$ $= 8.816 \div 2$ $= 4.408$	Think of $\div 200$ as $\div 100$ then $\div 2$ (or the other way around). Move the decimal point the required number of places to the left. Then divide by 2. State the answer.

When dividing a decimal number by another decimal number, we need to shift the decimal points in both numbers until the divisor becomes a whole number.

Example

Calculate $23.8 \div 0.05$.

✓ ***Solution***

Working	Explanation
$23.8 \div 0.05 = 238.0 \div 0.5$ $= 2380 \div 5$	Move the decimal point in both numbers 1 position to the right. Keep doing so until the divisor is a whole number.
$5\overline{)2380}$ = 476	Once 0.05 becomes 5, we can use short division to complete the calculation.

Example

Calculate $0.065 \div 0.004$.

✓ ***Solution***

Working	Explanation
$0.065 \div 0.004 = 0.65 \div 0.04$ $= 6.5 \div 0.4$ $= 65 \div 4$	Move the decimal point in both numbers 1 position to the right. Keep doing so until the divisor is a whole number.
$4\overline{)65.00}$ = 16.25	Once 0.004 becomes 4, we can use short division to complete the calculation.

Exercise 3.7.1

Calculate the following expressions.

a. $26.48 \div 8$ b. $4.23 \div 9$ c. $12.07 \div 4$ d. $5.205 \div 5$

e. $3.51 \div 4$ f. $1.79 \div 8$ g. $1.98 \div 2$ h. $6.324 \div 6$

Exercise 3.7.2

Calculate the following expressions.

a. $42.7 \div 100$ b. $5.56 \div 10$ c. $0.87 \div 10$

d. $68.02 \div 1000$ e. $2.532 \div 30$ f. $2.38 \div 70$

g. $2.82 \div 600$ h. $9.02 \div 1100$ i. $40.6 \div 8000$

Exercise 3.7.3

Calculate the following expressions.

a. $5.14 \div 0.2$ b. $10.2 \div 0.5$ c. $2.144 \div 0.08$

d. $9.96 \div 1.2$ e. $7.2 \div 0.003$ f. $1.16 \div 0.002$

g. $22.6 \div 0.04$ h. $1.32 \div 0.005$ i. $13.7 \div 0.08$

3.8 Decimals and fractions

To convert a fraction to a decimal we need to remember that the fraction bar is telling us to divide.

Example

Convert $\frac{1}{5}$ to a decimal number.

✓ Solution

Working	Explanation
$5\overline{)1.0}$	$\frac{1}{5} = 1 \div 5$
$\begin{array}{r} 0. \\ 5\overline{)\not{1}.^{1}0} \end{array}$	Set up short division as we do when dividing whole numbers. Keep the decimal points in line.
$\begin{array}{r} 0.2 \\ 5\overline{)\not{1}.^{1}0} \end{array}$	Begin the short division by asking how many 5s go into 1. Since 5 does not go into 1, the one unit becomes 10 tenths.
Therefore $\frac{1}{5} = 0.2$.	Repeat, following the steps previously mastered in short division. Once the decimal answer terminates, the conversion from fraction to decimal is complete.

Example

Convert $\frac{7}{8}$ to a decimal number.

✓ ***Solution***

Working	Explanation
$8\overline{)7.00}$ $\begin{array}{r} 0. \\ 8\overline{)\not{7}.{}^{7}00} \end{array}$ $\begin{array}{r} 0.8 \\ 8\overline{)\not{7}.{}^{7}0{}^{6}0} \end{array}$ $\begin{array}{r} 0.8\,7\,5 \\ 8\overline{)\not{7}.{}^{7}0{}^{6}0{}^{4}0} \end{array}$ Therefore $\frac{7}{8} = 0.875$.	$\frac{7}{8} = 7 \div 8$ Set up short division as we do when dividing whole numbers. Keep the decimal points in line. Begin the short division by asking how many 8s go into 7. Since 8 does not go into 7, the 7 units become 70 tenths. Repeat, following the steps previously mastered in short division. Once the decimal answer terminates, the conversion from fraction to decimal is complete.

Example

Convert $3\frac{1}{4}$ to a decimal number.

✓ ***Solution***

Working	Explanation
$4\overline{)1.00}$ $\begin{array}{r} 0.2 \\ 4\overline{)\not{1}.{}^{1}00} \end{array}$ $\begin{array}{r} 0.25 \\ 4\overline{)\not{1}.{}^{1}0{}^{2}0} \end{array}$	$3\frac{1}{4} = 3$ plus $1 \div 4$ Given that we already know that $1 \div 4 = 0.25$, we can combine the whole number and the decimal together to complete the conversion instantly. Or we can complete a short division as practised. $3\frac{1}{4} = 3.25$

To convert from decimals to fractions, we need to think about place values and write the number as a fraction with the denominator being a power of 10 where necessary. Simplify the fraction if possible.

Example

Convert 0.3 to a fraction.

✓ *Solution*

Working	Explanation
$0.3 = \frac{3}{10}$	0.3 is 3 tenths, which is the same as $\frac{3}{10}$. Given that $\frac{3}{10}$ is as simple as the fraction can be written, the conversion is complete.

Example

Convert 0.25 to a fraction.

✓ *Solution*

Working	Explanation
$\frac{25}{100} = \frac{1}{4}$	0.25 is the same as 25 hundredths. Or remember that 2 decimal places means that there should be 2 zeros in the denominator. Always simplify if possible. Refer back to the section on simplifying fractions if unsure.

Example

Convert 0.104 to a fraction.

✓ *Solution*

Working	Explanation
$\frac{104}{1000} = \frac{13}{25}$	0.104 is the same as 104 thousandths. Or remember that 3 decimal places means that there should be 3 zeros in the denominator. Always simplify if possible. Refer back to the section of simplifying fractions if unsure.

Exercise 3.8.1

Convert the following fractions to decimals.

a. $\frac{3}{4}$ b. $\frac{3}{5}$ c. $\frac{1}{8}$ d. $\frac{7}{20}$

e. $\frac{5}{8}$ f. $\frac{3}{20}$ g. $\frac{3}{25}$ h. $\frac{43}{50}$

i. $\frac{3}{10}$ j. $\frac{9}{40}$ k. $\frac{3}{2}$ l. $\frac{5}{4}$

m. $\frac{11}{2}$ n. $\frac{9}{5}$ o. $\frac{53}{20}$

Exercise 3.8.2

Convert the following decimals to fractions, giving the final answer in its simplest form.

a. 0.7 b. 0.12 c. 0.05 d. 0.15

e. 2.5 f. 0.420 g. 0.625 h. 1.3

i. 0.325 j. 3.6

Answers

Exercise 3.1

a. seven tenths b. seven thousandths c. seven hundredths

d. seven ten-thousandths e. seven thousandths f. seven tenths

g. seven hundredths h. seven ten-thousandths

Exercise 3.2

a. $0.65 > 0.57$ b. $2.4 > 0.42$ c. $0.303 < 0.333$

d. $2.32 > 1.955$ e. $4.70 = 4.7$ f. $0.08 < 0.80$

Exercise 3.3

a. 4.9 b. 6.7 c. 7.64 d. 4.55

e. 0.642 f. 6.36 g. 4.3 h. 0.707

Exercise 3.4.1

a. 8.98 b. 18 c. 7.81 d. 6.524

Exercise 3.4.2

a. 2.24 b. 3.49 c. 2.63 d. 3.31

Exercise 3.5.1

a. 824 b. 71.12 c. 3510 d. 2100

Exercise 3.5.2

a. 427 b. 6630 c. 30 012 d. 435

Exercise 3.6

a. 0.18 b. 0.072 c. 0.07 d. 0.0165
e. 1.28 f. 1.02 g. 25.42 h. 0.84

Exercise 3.7.1

a. 3.31 b. 0.47 c. 3.0175 d. 1.041
e. 0.8775 f. 0.22375 g. 0.99 h. 1.054

Exercise 3.7.2

a. 0.427 b. 0.556 c. 0.087 d. 0.06802
e. 0.0844 f. 0.034 g. 0.0047 h. 0.0082
i. 0.005075

Exercise 3.7.3

a. 25.7 b. 20.4 c. 26.8 d. 8.3
e. 2400 f. 580 g. 565 h. 264
i. 171.25

Exercise 3.8.1

a. 0.75 b. 0.6 c. 0.125 d. 0.35
e. 0.625 f. 0.15 g. 0.12 h. 0.86
i. 0.3 j. 0.225 k. 1.5 l. 1.25
m. 5.5 n. 1.8 o. 2.65

Exercise 3.8.2

a. $\frac{7}{10}$ b. $\frac{3}{25}$ c. $\frac{1}{20}$ d. $\frac{3}{20}$
e. $\frac{5}{2}$ f. $\frac{21}{50}$ g. $\frac{5}{8}$ h. $\frac{13}{10}$
i. $\frac{13}{40}$ j. $\frac{18}{5}$

Chapter 4 – Percentages, money and time

Per cent means 'out of 100', therefore 16% means '16 out of 100'. We can also understand 100% is a **whole**.

Any fraction, decimal or whole number can be expressed as a percentage, but it must include the percentage sign (%) to make it clear that it represents a value out of 100.

4.1 Decimals and percentages

We can convert between decimals and percentages by moving the decimal point.

To convert from a decimal to a percentage, move the decimal point 2 places to the right.

$$0.25 = 25\%$$

It is not necessary to write a decimal point after 25, but percentages can have decimal places.

To convert from a percentage to a decimal, move the decimal point 2 places to the left.

$$36.7\% = 0.367$$

Example

Convert the following decimals to percentages and percentages to decimals.

a. 0.05 **b.** 0.704 **c.** 60% **d.** 4%

✓ *Solution*

Working	Explanation
a. $0.05 = 5\%$	Move the decimal point 2 places to the right and add a percentage sign.
b. $0.704 = 70.4\%$	Move the decimal point 2 places to the right and add a percentage sign.
c. $60\% = 0.6$	Move the decimal point 2 places to the left and remove the percentage sign.
d. $4\% = 0.04$	Move the decimal point 2 places to the left and remove the percentage sign.

Exercise 4.1.1

Convert the following decimals to percentages.

a. 0.5 **b.** 0.75 **c.** 0.8 **d.** 0.006

e. 0.903 **f.** 0.03 **g.** 2.4 **h.** 1

Exercise 4.1.2

Convert the following percentages to decimals.

a. 30% **b.** 80% **c.** 99% **d.** 68%

e. 1% **f.** 2% **g.** 0.5% **h.** 120%

4.2 Percentage of an amount

There are many ways to find the percentage of a number or amount. We will explore two main ways. The first way requires an understanding that **per cent** means 'out of 100', so a percentage can be written as a part of a whole.

One way to find the percentage of a number or amount is as follows.

- Express the required percentage as a fraction.
- Change the 'of' to a multiplication sign.
- Express the number as a fraction.
- Multiply the two fractions and simplify.

However, it may be easier to use mental strategies.

- 10% of any number can be found by shifting the decimal point 1 place left.
- 1% of any number can be found by shifting the decimal point 2 places left.
- We can add and multiply these strategies to get to the required percentage.

Example

Calculate 40% of 120.

✓ Solution

Working	Explanation
$40\% \text{ of } 120 = \frac{40}{100} \times \frac{120}{1}$ $= \frac{4\cancel{0}}{1\cancel{0}\cancel{0}} \times \frac{12\cancel{0}}{1}$ $= 48$	Express the percentage as a fraction. Change 'of' to ×. Express the whole number as a fraction with a denominator of 1. Simplify and then multiply.

Example

Calculate 2% of 250.

✓ Solution

Working	Explanation
2% of 250 $\times 2$ ($1\% = 2.5$ → $2\% = 5$) $\times 2$	Move the decimal point 2 places to the left to find 1% of 250. Multiply by 2 to find 2%.

Exercise 4.2

Calculate the following using one of the methods discussed previously.

a. 8% of 300 **b.** 15% of 80 **c.** 25% of \$440

d. 12% of 150 **e.** 3% of \$125 **f.** 11% of \$55

g. 49% of 600 **h.** 61% of \$1200

4.3 Fractions, decimals and percentages

There are a number of ways to convert between fractions, decimals and percentages. You should be aware that one method may be easier than another. For example, although the answer is the same, calculating $\frac{1}{8}$ of 80 is easier than calculating 12.5% of 80.

The charts below are helpful conversion guides for some common decimals, fractions and percentages.

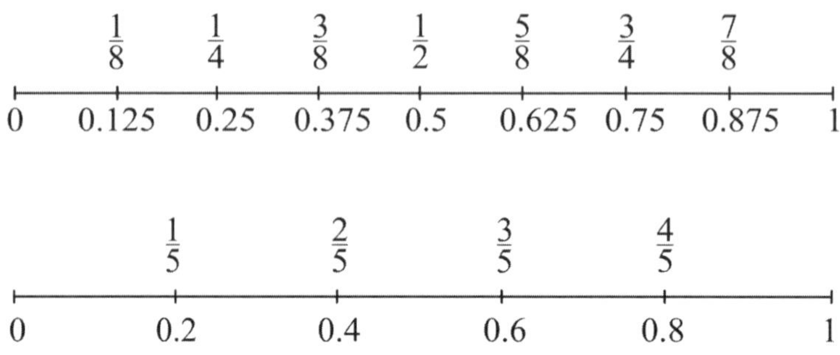

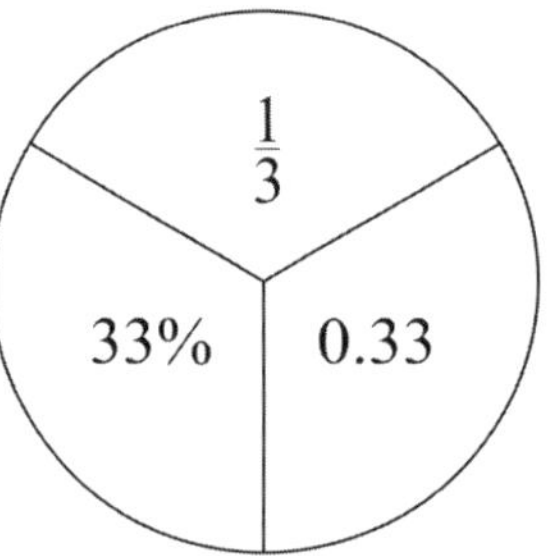

Example

Complete the following conversion table.

	Percentage	Fraction	Decimal
a.	20%	?	?
b.	?	$\frac{11}{20}$	?
c.	?	?	0.06

✓ *Solution*

Working	Explanation
a. $\frac{2\not{0}}{10\not{0}} = \frac{1}{5} = 0.2$	Write 20% as a fraction of 100 and then simplify it. Use one of the charts to convert the fraction to a decimal.
b. $\frac{11}{20} \overset{\times 5}{=} \frac{55}{100} = 55\% = 0.55$ (× 5 on the numerator and on the denominator)	Find an equivalent fraction with a denominator of 100. This can easily be converted to a percentage. Convert the percentage to a decimal by moving the decimal point 2 places to the left.
c. $0.06 = 6\% = \frac{6}{100} = \frac{3}{50}$	Move the decimal point 2 places to the right to convert the decimal to a percentage. Write 6% as a fraction of 100 and then simplify it.

✎ Exercise 4.3.1

Complete the following conversion table.

Percentage	Fraction	Decimal
30%	?	?
?	$\frac{9}{20}$	?
?	?	0.58

✎ Exercise 4.3.2

a. Express 16 as a percentage of 20.

b. Express 20 cents as a percentage of \$4.00.

c. Express 45 minutes as a percentage of 1 hour.

4.4 Financial mathematics

The most challenging aspect of financial mathematics is not the maths; it is the words in the problems and understanding what the question is asking. In this section we cover the main concepts of Year 7 financial maths.

Example

Calculate the sale price of a jacket that had a discount of 20% on the original price of $300.

✓ *Solution*

Working	Explanation
20% of $300 $\frac{20}{1\cancel{00}} \times \frac{3\cancel{00}}{1} = \$60$	Calculate the dollar amount of the discount first.
$300 - 60 = \$240$	Then we use the equation **original price – discount = sale price** to find the answer. Always write the final answer with a dollar sign.

Example

Kym buys 4 kg of oranges for $18.40. What was the price per kilogram?

✓ *Solution*

Working	Explanation
$4\overline{)18.{}^{2}40}$ = 4.60 The price is $4.60/kg.	The word 'per' is referring to a rate. All rates should be written as a value of a single unit ($/kg).

Example

A sausage sizzle generated $1230 of sales. If the cost of setting up the sizzle was $344, how much profit was made?

✓ Solution

Working	Explanation
$1230 - 344 = \$886$	'Sales' is the same as income, so use the equation **income – cost = profit** to find the answer.

Exercise 4.4

a. A 4-litre container of milk costs $13.20. What is the cost per 100 mL?

b. Jesse sells flowers at a market stall. One day she takes in $895 from the sale of flowers. If the flowers cost Jesse $300 and she had to pay a fee of $50 to rent the stall, what profit did she make for the day?

c. Cailin's bank account balance was $710.20 just before she withdrew $55.65 to pay a bill. How much did she have left in her account after the withdrawal?

d. Mat fills his car with petrol at a cost of $1.90 per litre. If he buys 80 litres, how much must he pay?

e. Notebooks cost $3.17 each. What is the cost of four notebooks?

f. A couch is advertised in a furniture sale catalogue at the discounted price of $999, a saving of $350. Find the original price of the couch.

4.5 Time

As with fractions, decimals and percentages, it is useful to be able to convert between units of time.

The chart below is a helpful conversion guide.

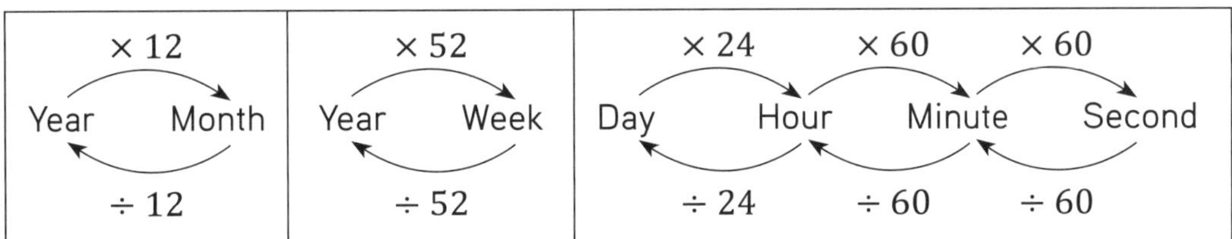

Example

Use the conversion chart above to convert 440 minutes to hours and minutes.

✓ Solution

Working	Explanation
$6\overline{)44.{}^{2}0}$ = $7.\dot{3}$ 7 hours, 20 minutes.	There are 60 minutes in an hour, so divide 440 by 60. It will be easier if you simplify first: $44\not{0} \div 6\not{0}$ The result is $7.\dot{3}$ hours. Note that $0.\dot{3}$ is the same as $\frac{1}{3}$ and $\frac{1}{3}$ of an hour is 20 minutes.

Example

Use the conversion chart on the previous page to convert 42 hours to days and hours.

✓ Solution

Working	Explanation
$\frac{42}{24} = \frac{7}{4}$ $4\overline{)7.{}^{3}0{}^{2}0}$ = 1.75 1 day, 18 hours.	There are 24 hours in a day, so divide 42 by 24. It will be easier if you simplify first. The result is 1.75 days. Note that 0.75 is the same as $\frac{3}{4}$ and $\frac{3}{4}$ of a day is $\frac{3}{4} \times 24 = 18$ hours.

Exercise 4.5

a. Convert 65 weeks into years and weeks.

b. Convert 48 months into years.

c. Convert 1 day into minutes.

d. Just before a music lesson Anna has a spelling test that lasts 20 minutes. The music lesson lasts for 50 minutes and ends at 10.30 am.

  i. What time does the music lesson start?

  ii. What time does Anna start the spelling test?

e. On Saturday John spent 4 hours and 20 minutes studying. On Sunday he spent 2 hours and 45 minutes studying. How long in total did John study? Give your answer in hours and minutes.

Answers

Exercise 4.1.1

a. 50%
b. 75%
c. 80%
d. 0.6%
e. 90.3%
f. 3%
g. 240%
h. 100%

Exercise 4.1.2

a. 0.3
b. 0.8
c. 0.99
d. 0.68
e. 0.01
f. 0.02
g. 0.005
h. 1.2

Exercise 4.2

a. 24
b. 12
c. $110
d. 18
e. $3.75
f. $6.05
g. 294
h. $732

Exercise 4.3.1

Percentage	Fraction	Decimal
30%	$\frac{3}{10}$	0.3
45%	$\frac{9}{20}$	0.45
58%	$\frac{29}{50}$	0.58

Exercise 4.3.2

a. 80%
b. 5%
c. 75%

Exercise 4.4

a. 33 cents
b. $545
c. $654.55
d. $152
e. $12.68
f. $1349

Exercise 4.5

a. 1 year, 13 weeks
b. 4 years
c. 1440 minutes
d. i. 9.40 am
   ii. 9.20 am
e. 7 hours and 5 minutes

Chapter 5 – Negative numbers

We need negative numbers to represent the opposite of positive numbers.

Negative numbers can be whole numbers, decimals or fractions.

5.1 Integers

Integers are whole numbers.

Any whole number larger than zero is a **positive integer**.

Any whole number less than zero is a **negative integer**.

Zero is the only integer that is neither positive nor negative.

We can use a number line or a Cartesian axis to represent positive and negative integers.

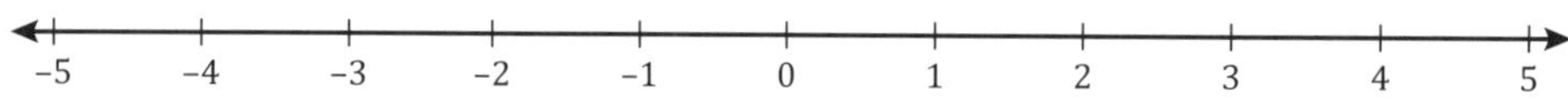

Example

Write an integer to represent each of the following.

a. a temperature of 12 degrees below zero

b. a distance of 5 metres

c. owing $10

d. 2 floors below ground level

✓ Solution

Working	Explanation
a. -12	When a temperature is 'below zero', it means that it is a negative value.
b. 5	Distance is always a positive number, as it refers to a length. (Direction can be negative, but not distance.)
c. -10	In financial maths, owing money (that is, a debt) is a negative value.
d. -2	Think of ground level as zero, so any level below it is a negative level.

Example

Write the coordinates of each point marked on the grid below.

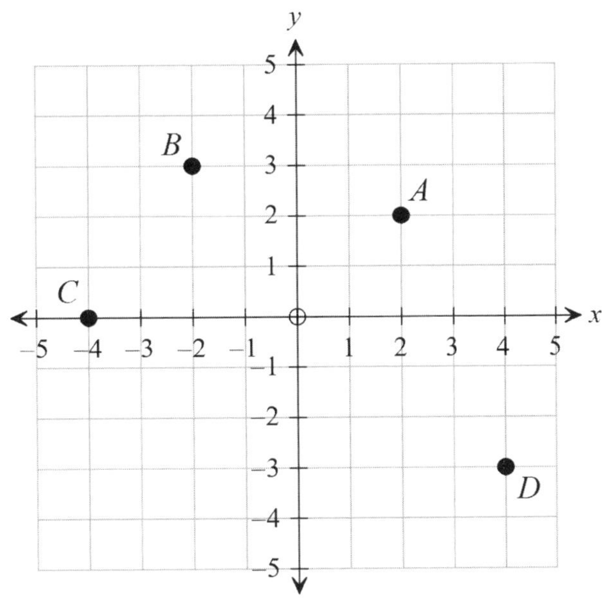

✓ ***Solution***

Working	Explanation
$A(2, 2)$ $B(-2, 3)$ $C(-4, 0)$ $D(4, -3)$	The x-axis is the horizontal number line, with positive numbers to the right of 0 and negative numbers to the left of 0. The y-axis is the vertical axis, with positive numbers above 0 and negative numbers below 0. Remember to start at the origin and go across and then up or down, so that the coordinates are the x-value followed by the y-value.

Exercise 5.1.1

Write an integer to represent the following.

a. the fifth storey of an apartment building

b. a fridge temperature of 4 degrees Celsius

c. a freezer temperature of 17 degrees Celsius below zero

d. a half-full 2-litre milk bottle

Exercise 5.1.2

Write the coordinates of each point marked on the grid below.

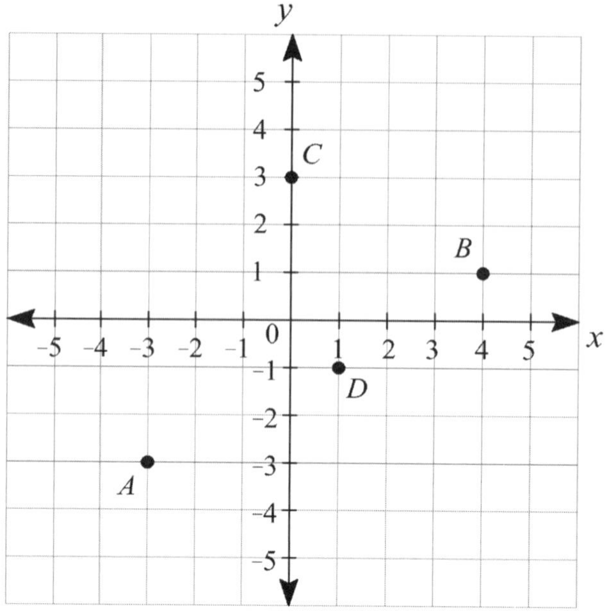

5.2 Comparing and ordering integers

Before solving problems involving integers, we must be confident in ordering and comparing them. Remember, **descending order** means going down and **ascending order** means going up.

Example

Write the next two terms that continue the following pattern.

$$-15, -11, -7, -3, \_\_, \_\_$$

✓ *Solution*

Working	Explanation
$-15, -11, -7, -3, \underline{1}, \underline{5}$	Each of the given numbers is increasing by $+4$, so continue the pattern by adding the next two numbers that increase by $+4$.

Example

Insert > (greater than) or < (less than) in the empty box to make the following statement true.

$$-2 \square -7$$

✓ ***Solution***

Working	Explanation
$-2 \boxed{>} -7$	If we mark both numbers on a number line, we can see that -2 is further right than -7, so -2 is greater than -7. -8 -7 -6 -5 -4 -3 -2 -1 0 1 2 3

Example

Arrange the integers 5, -1, 0, 2 and -4 in descending order.

✓ ***Solution***

Working	Explanation
$5, 2, 0, -1, -4$	Placing the numbers on a number line can help us quickly see the descending order, as descending order goes from right to left on a number line. -6 -5 -4 -3 -2 -1 0 1 2 3 4 5 6

Exercise 5.2.1

Write the next two terms to continue each of the following patterns.

a. $-18, -13, -8, -3,$ __, __ **b.** $5, 1, -3, -7,$ __, __ **c.** $-23, -20, -17, -14,$ __, __

Exercise 5.2.2

Insert > (greater than) or < (less than) in each of the following empty boxes to make the statement true.

a. $-9 \square -11$ **b.** $-6 \square -3$ **c.** $-1 \square -2$ **d.** $-22 \square -19$

Exercise 5.2.3

Arrange the following integers in descending order.

a. $6, 4, -2, 0, -11$ **b.** $-13, -3, -4, 2, -11$ **c.** $-16, -8, -24, 1, 2$

5.3 Addition and subtraction of integers

When adding or subtracting a negative number, there are rules that we must follow. For example:

- Adding a negative number is the same as subtracting a positive number.
- Subtracting a negative number is the same as adding a positive number.

Example

Evaluate the following integer expressions.

a. $9+(-3)$ b. $5-(-4)$ c. $-6-2$

✓ Solution

Working	Explanation
a. $9+(-3)=9-3$ $=6$	Adding a negative number is the same as subtracting a positive number.
b. $5-(-4)=5+4$ $=9$	Subtracting a negative number is the same as adding a positive number.
c. $-6-2=-(6+2)$ $=-8$	Where subtraction involves two negative numbers, ignore the signs, add the numbers and make the final answer negative.

In calculations where there is a positive and a negative number, ignore the signs and find the difference between the two. The final answer will have the same sign as whichever digit is further from zero.

Example

Evaluate the following integer expressions.

a. $-4+10$ b. $-12+4$ c. $3-7$

✓ Solution

Working	Explanation
a. $-4+10=6$	The difference between 4 and 10 is 6. 10 is further from 0 than -4, so the answer is positive.
b. $-12+4=-8$	The difference between 12 and 4 is 8. -12 is further from 0 than 4, so the answer is negative.
c. $3-7=-4$	The difference between 3 and 7 is 4. -7 is further from 0 than 3, so the answer is negative.

Exercise 5.3

Evaluate the following integer expressions.

a. $10 + (-4)$ b. $14 + (-6)$ c. $8 + (-15)$ d. $2 + (-13)$ e. $5 - (-9)$

f. $6 - (-2)$ g. $5 - (+3)$ h. $9 - (+6)$ i. $-4 - 7$ j. $-10 - 23$

k. $-4 - 4$ l. $-7 + 1$ m. $-9 + 13$ n. $14 - 22$ o. $11 - 30$

5.4 Multiplication and division of integers

When two numbers with the same sign are multiplied or divided, the result will be a positive number.

When two numbers with different signs are multiplied or divided, the result will be a negative number.

Example

Evaluate the following integer expressions.

a. -8×3 b. -5×-6 c. $-32 \div 8$ d. $-45 \div -9$

✓ *Solution*

Working	Explanation
a. $-8 \times 3 = -24$	Given that the 8 is negative and the 3 is positive, the final product will be negative.
b. $-5 \times -6 = 30$	Given that both the 5 and the 6 are negative, the final product will be positive.
c. $-32 \div 8 = -4$	Given that the 32 is negative and the 8 is positive, the final quotient will be negative.
d. $-45 \div -9 = 5$	Given that both the 45 and the 9 are negative, the final quotient will be positive.

Exercise 5.4

Evaluate the following integer expressions.

a. 9×-2 b. -7×7 c. -10×-3 d. -2×-11

e. $-15 \div 3$ f. $63 \div -7$ g. $-99 \div -3$ h. $-16 \div -16$

5.5 Powers of integers

Squares, cubes and other powers can be calculated for both positive and negative integers.

Example

Evaluate the following integer expressions.

a. 3^2 **b.** $(-5)^2$ **c.** -5^2 **d.** $(-2)^4$

✓ *Solution*

Working	Explanation
a. $3^2 = 3 \times 3$ $= 9$	Squaring an integer (power 2) is the same as multiplying the number by itself.
b. $(-5)^2 = -5 \times -5$ $= 25$	When squaring a negative integer, brackets matter. If the negative sign is inside the bracket, it is the same as multiplying the number by itself.
c. $-5^2 = -(5 \times 5)$ $= -25$	If there are no brackets, square the negative integer as if it were a positive integer and place a negative sign in front of the product.
d. $(-2)^4 = -2 \times -2 \times -2 \times -2$ $= 16$	Raising a number to the power 4 is very similar to squaring except that this time you multiply the number by itself 4 times.

Exercise 5.5

Evaluate the following integer expressions.

a. 4^2 **b.** -4^2 **c.** $(-4)^2$ **d.** -2^3

e. $(-2)^3$ **f.** -9^2 **g.** -7^2 **h.** $(-3)^3$

5.6 Negative fractions

Negative fractions can be added, subtracted, multiplied and divided in the same way as negative integers.

In some cases it may be helpful to place negative fractions on a number line before a calculation. The following number lines may help you see where a negative fraction should be placed.

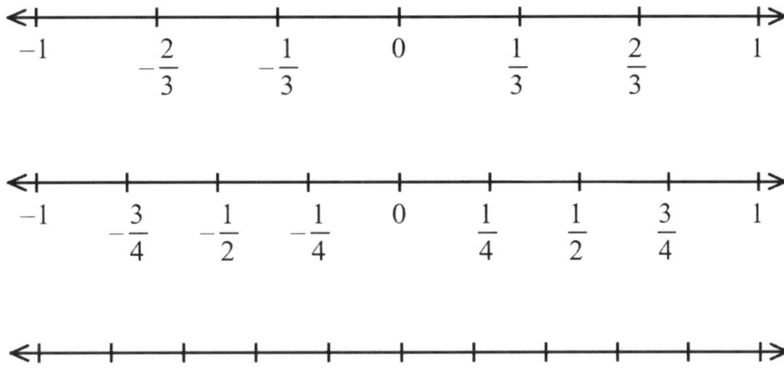

Example

Evaluate $-\frac{1}{2} + \frac{2}{3}$.

✓ Solution

Working	Explanation
$-\frac{1}{2} + \frac{2}{3} = -\frac{3}{6} + \frac{4}{6}$ $= \frac{1}{6}$	The approach is the same as when adding positive fractions: convert each fraction to an equivalent fraction so that each has the same denominator. Then add the numerators using the techniques discussed in section 5.3.

Example

Evaluate $-\frac{3}{4} - \frac{2}{5}$.

✓ Solution

Working	Explanation
$-\frac{3}{4} - \frac{2}{5} = -\frac{15}{20} - \frac{8}{20}$ $= -\frac{23}{20}$	The approach is the same as when subtracting positive fractions: convert each fraction to an equivalent fraction so that each has the same denominator. Then find the difference between the numerators using the techniques discussed in section 5.3.

Example

Evaluate $-\frac{2}{7} \times -\frac{3}{5}$.

✓ Solution

Working	Explanation
$-\frac{2}{7} \times -\frac{3}{5} = \frac{2 \times 3}{7 \times 5}$ $= \frac{6}{35}$	The approach is the same as when multiplying positive fractions. Given that both fractions are negative, the product will be positive.

Example

Evaluate $-\frac{5}{6} \div \frac{7}{12}$.

✓ Solution

Working	Explanation
$-\frac{5}{6} \div \frac{7}{12} = -\frac{5}{6} \times \frac{12}{7}$ $= -\frac{5}{{}_{1}\cancel{6}} \times \frac{\cancel{12}^{2}}{7}$ $= -\frac{10}{7}$	The approach is the same as when dividing positive fractions: keep the first fraction the same, change the division symbol to multiplication and flip the second fraction to create its reciprocal. Always try to simplify before multiplying. Given that one fraction is negative and the other positive, the quotient will be negative.

Exercise 5.6

Evaluate the following expressions involving fractions.

a. $-\frac{3}{4} + \frac{1}{5}$

b. $\frac{2}{5} - \frac{7}{3}$

c. $-\frac{4}{3} - \frac{3}{2}$

d. $-\frac{2}{7} - 1$

e. $\frac{7}{2} \times -\frac{1}{14}$

f. $-\frac{2}{3} \times -\frac{12}{5}$

g. $-\frac{2}{7} \div \frac{1}{3}$

h. $-\frac{1}{2} \div -\frac{2}{1}$

5.7 Negative decimals

Negative decimals can be added, subtracted, multiplied and divided in the same way as negative integers.

We can apply the rules for operations with negative integers and the rules for operations with decimals together.

Example

Evaluate $-0.3 - 1.4$.

✓ ***Solution***

Working	Explanation
$-0.3 - 1.4 = -(0.3 + 1.4)$ $= -1.7$	In calculations involving the difference of two negative decimals, ignore the signs, add the decimals and make the final answer negative.

Example

Evaluate -0.6×-0.3.

✓ ***Solution***

Working	Explanation
$-0.6 \times -0.3 = 0.18$	Given that both 0.6 and 0.3 are negative, the final product will be positive. If you are unsure about the process for multiplying decimals, see section 3.6.

Example

Evaluate $-0.8 \div -0.2$.

✓ ***Solution***

Working	Explanation
$-0.8 \div -0.2 = -8 \div -2$ $= 4$	Given that both 0.8 and 0.2 are negative, the final quotient will be positive. If you are unsure about the process for dividing decimals, see section 3.7.

Example

Evaluate $(-0.6)^2$.

✓ Solution

Working	Explanation
$(-0.6)^2 = -0.6 \times -0.6$ $= 0.36$	A negative decimal is inside brackets, so multiply it by itself. The product will be positive. If you are unsure about the process for multiplying decimals, see section 3.6.

Exercise 5.7

Evaluate the following decimal expressions.

a. $-0.25 - 0.9$ **b.** $-0.4 + 0.75$ **c.** -0.55×-0.2 **d.** 0.4×-1.2

e. $-0.9 \div 0.2$ **f.** $0.4 \div -8$ **g.** -0.5^2 **h.** $(-1.1)^2$

Answers

Exercise 5.1.1

a. 5 b. 4 c. -17 d. 1

Exercise 5.1.2

$A(-3, -3)$, $B(4, 1)$, $C(0, 3)$, $D(1, -1)$

Exercise 5.2.1

a. $-18, -13, -8, -3, \underline{2}, \underline{7}$ b. $5, 1, -3, -7, \underline{-11}, \underline{-15}$

c. $-23, -20, -17, -14, \underline{-11}, \underline{-8}$

Exercise 5.2.2

a. $-9 > -11$ b. $-6 < -3$ c. $-1 > -2$ d. $-22 < -19$

Exercise 5.2.3

a. $6, 4, 0, -2, -11$ b. $2, -3, -4, -11, -13$

c. $2, 1, -8, -16, -24$

Exercise 5.3

a. 6 b. 8 c. -7 d. -11 e. 14

f. 8 g. 2 h. 3 i. -11 j. -33

k. -8 l. -6 m. 4 n. -8 o. -19

Exercise 5.4

a. -18
b. -49
c. 30
d. 22
e. -5
f. -9
g. 33
h. 1

Exercise 5.5

a. 16
b. -16
c. 16
d. -8
e. -8
f. -81
g. -49
h. -27

Exercise 5.6

a. $-\frac{11}{20}$
b. $-\frac{29}{15}$
c. $-\frac{17}{6}$
d. $-\frac{9}{7}$
e. $-\frac{1}{4}$
f. $\frac{8}{5}$
g. $-\frac{6}{7}$
h. $\frac{1}{4}$

Exercise 5.7

a. -1.15
b. 0.35
c. 0.11
d. -0.48
e. -4.5
f. -0.05
g. -0.25
h. 1.21

Chapter 6 – Multiples, factors, powers and roots

6.1 Multiples

A multiple is the **product** of a number and another number. For example, 5, 10 and 15 are all multiples of 5.

$$1 \times 5 = 5 \qquad 2 \times 5 = 10 \qquad 3 \times 5 = 15$$

Multiples can also be found by skip counting. For example, the following are multiples of 5.

$$5, 10, 15, 20, 25, \ldots$$

If we write the multiples of two numbers and a number appears in both lists, we call that number a **common** multiple. For example, 20 is a common multiple of 5 and 10. The lists may have more than one common multiple.

Example

a. Write down the first five multiples of 8.

b. Find the fourth multiple of 6.

c. Show that 24 is the lowest common multiple of 8 and 6.

✓ *Solution*

Working	Explanation
a. $8, 16, 24, 32, 40$	Starting with the initial multiple, 8, increase by 8 repeatedly until you have five multiples. **Note**: a number is a multiple of itself.
b. $6, 12, 18, 24$	Starting with the initial multiple, 6, increase by 6 repeatedly. 24 is the fourth multiple of 6.
c. $8, 16, \boxed{24}, 32, 40$ $6, 12, 18, \boxed{24}, 30, 36$	By writing the multiples of both 8 and 6, we can see that the lowest number that appears in both lists is 24.

Exercise 6.1.1

Find the lowest common multiple of the following pairs of numbers.

a. 7 and 8 **b.** 10 and 12 **c.** 16 and 24

Exercise 6.1.2

A phone application flashes two different lights. One flashes every 25 seconds and the other flashes every minute. Determine the first three times that they flash together after the application is started.

Exercise 6.1.3

Write the first number that is odd, greater than 40 and a multiple of 9.

6.2 Factors

If two or more numbers divide exactly into another number (that is, there is no remainder) they are said to be factors of that number. For example, 3, 5, 6 and 10 are all factors of 30.

$30 \div 5 = 6$ $\qquad$ $30 \div 10 = 3$

If you list the factors of one number and list the factors of another number, a factor that is in both lists is called a **common factor**.

Example

a. Find the factors of 20 and write them in ascending order.

b. Find the factors of 30 and write them in ascending order.

c. Determine the highest common factor of 20 and 30.

✓ *Solution*

Working	Explanation
a. $1 \times 20 \quad 2 \times 10 \quad 4 \times 5$	Using our understanding of the multiplication tables we can write the factors as products.
$1, 2, 4, 5, 10, 20$	Write the factors in ascending order (smallest to largest).
b. $1 \times 30 \quad 2 \times 15 \quad 3 \times 10 \quad 5 \times 6$	Using our understanding of the multiplication tables we can write the factors as products.
$1, 2, 3, 5, 6, 10, 15, 30$	Write the factors in ascending order (smallest to largest).
c. $1, 2, 4, 5, \boxed{10}, 20$ $1, 2, 3, 5, 6, \boxed{10}, 15, 30$	After listing the factors of 20 and then 30, we can compare both lists. We see that 10 is the largest number in both lists. Therefore 10 is the highest common factor of 20 and 30. **Note**: the highest common factor is also called the greatest common divisor.

Exercise 6.2.1

List all the factors of the following numbers in ascending order.

a. 16 **b.** 28 **c.** 50 **d.** 72

Exercise 6.2.2

Find the highest common factor of the following pairs of numbers.

a. 24 and 30 **b.** 16 and 64 **c.** 15 and 25 **d.** 27 and 45

6.3 Divisibility

We often want to know whether a large number can be divided into a smaller number with no remainder without having to do long division or short division.

We can check for divisibility using the following properties of numbers.

Divisibility tests	
$\left\{\begin{array}{l}2\\4\\8\end{array}\right.$	A number is divisible by 2 if it ends in 0, 2, 4, 6 or 8. A number is divisible by 4 if the last two digits are divisible by 4. A number is divisible by 8 if the last three digits are divisible by 8.
$\left\{\begin{array}{l}3\\6\\9\end{array}\right.$	A number is divisible by 3 if the sum of its digits is divisible by 3. A number is divisible by 6 if it is divisible by 2 and 3. A number is divisible by 9 if the sum of its digits is divisible by 9.
$\left\{\begin{array}{l}5\\10\end{array}\right.$	A number is divisible by 5 if it ends in 0 or 5. A number is divisible by 10 if it ends in 0.

Note: there are other tests of divisibility, but the ones listed above are the most common.

Example

Fill in the blank squares in $5\square231\square$ with a digit between 0 and 9 to make the number

a. divisible by 4 **b.** divisible by 6 **c.** divisible by 5.

✓ *Solution*

Working	Explanation
a. $5\square231\boxed{2}$ $5\square231\boxed{6}$	The first square can be any value because, for a number to be divisible by 4, only the last two digits must be divisible by 4. There are only two solutions for the last digit.
b. One solution is $5\boxed{1}231\boxed{0}$	For a number to be divisible by 6, it must be divisible by 2 (that is, end in 0, 2, 4, 6 or 8) and divisible by 3 (that is, the sum of its digits must be divisible by 3). There are many solutions.
c. $5\square231\boxed{0}$ $5\square231\boxed{5}$	The first box can be any value because, for a number to be divisible by 5, the only requirement is that the last digit must be 0 or 5. There are two solutions for the last digit.

Exercise 6.3

a. Show that 6732 is divisible by 9 and 4.

b. Write the number that is divisible by 6 and is closest to 50.

c. Write the number that is even, divisible by 3 and between 20 and 30.

6.4 Powers and roots

A **square number** is a number that is produced when we multiply a number by itself.

The number 36 is a square number because $36 = 6 \times 6$.

We can also write this as $36 = 6^2$, where the power (2) can be read as 'squared'.

Finding the **square root** of a number is the opposite of squaring a number. So the square root of 36 is 6.

The mathematical symbol for square root is $\sqrt{\ }$, as in $\sqrt{36} = 6$.

Just as we can write 6×6 as 6^2, we can write $6 \times 6 \times 6 \times 6 \times 6$ as 6^5, which can be read as '6 to the power of 5'.

We say that 6^5 is written in **index form**, where 6 is the base, and 5 is the index or power.

When a number written in index form is converted to the base number multiplied by itself a number of times, we say that the number has been converted to **expanded form**. For example, 6^5 in expanded form is $6 \times 6 \times 6 \times 6 \times 6$.

Example

a. Evaluate $\sqrt{64}$ and $\sqrt{121}$.

b. Write $3 \times 3 \times 3 \times 3$ in index form.

c. Write 8^3 in expanded form.

✓ *Solution*

Working	Explanation
a. $\sqrt{64} = 8$ $\sqrt{121} = 11$	From the multiplication tables, we know that $8 \times 8 = 64$ $11 \times 11 = 121$ So the square root of 64 is 8 and the square root of 121 is 11.
b. $3 \times 3 \times 3 \times 3 = 3^4$	The number of 3s being multiplied together is the value of the power (4) when written in index form.
c. $8^3 = 8 \times 8 \times 8$	The power in index form becomes the number of the base values that are multiplied together.

Exercise 6.4

a. Evaluate the following expressions.

i. 4^2 ii. 7^2 iii. 2^3 iv. $\sqrt{100}$ v. $\sqrt{49}$

b. Write each of the following in index form.

i. $4 \times 4 \times 4 \times 4$ ii. 6×6

c. Evaluate $3^2 \times 2^2$.

6.5 Prime and composite numbers

The most important numbers in our natural number system are **prime numbers**. Prime numbers are divisible by only themselves and 1. They have no other factors.

Composite numbers have factors other than themselves and 1.

The set of prime numbers begins

$$2, 3, 5, 7, 11, 13, 17, 19, 23, 29, 31, 37, 41, 43, 47, 53, 59 \ldots$$

The set of composite numbers begins

$$4, 6, 8, 9, 10, 12, 14, 15, 16, 18, 20, 21, 22 \ldots$$

Note: the number 1 is regarded as neither prime nor composite, because it has only one factor. Also note that, except for 2, all prime numbers are odd numbers.

When multiplied together, prime numbers can make any **composite number**. Another way of saying this is that any number can be expanded into factors that are prime numbers. In fact, every number has only one unique set of prime factors.

Example

Write 42 as a product of its prime factors in expanded form.

✓ *Solution*

Working	Explanation
(42) → 6, (7); 6 → (2), (3) $42 = 2 \times 3 \times 7$	We can list all the factors of 42 and note those that are prime. Alternatively, we can create a factor tree and circle the prime factors.

Example

Write 60 as a product of its prime factors in expanded form.

✓ ***Solution***

Working	Explanation
60 6 10 2 3 2 5 $60 = 2 \times 2 \times 3 \times 5$	We can list all the factors of 60 and note those that are prime. Alternatively, we can create a factor tree and circle the prime factors.

Example

Find the highest common factor and lowest common multiple of 42 and 60 by examining the prime factors of both numbers.

✓ ***Solution***

Working	Explanation
$42 = \not{2} \times \not{3} \times \underline{7}$ $60 = \not{2} \times \underline{2} \times \not{3} \times \underline{5}$ $\text{HCF} = 2 \times 3$ $\text{LCM} = 6 \times \underline{2} \times \underline{5} \times \underline{7}$	Collect any pairs of primes that appear in both factorisations. In this case, 2 and 3 are factors of both 42 and 60. The product of these factors will be the highest common factor (HCF). The product of the remaining prime factors and the HCF will be the lowest common multiple (LCM). The highest common factor of 42 and 60 is 6, and the lowest common multiple is 420.

Exercise 6.5.1

Write the following numbers as a product of their prime factors in index form.

a. 36 **b.** 50 **c.** 124 **d.** 75

Exercise 6.5.2

Determine the number that is given by the following prime factorisations.

a. $2^2 \times 4^2$ **b.** 5×7^2

Exercise 6.5.3

Determine the highest common factor and lowest common multiple of the following pairs of numbers.

a. 14 and 32 **b.** 24 and 56

Answers

Exercise 6.1.1

a. 56   b. 60   c. 48

Exercise 6.1.2

5 minutes, 10 minutes, and 15 minutes.

Exercise 6.1.3

45

Exercise 6.2.1

a. 1, 2, 4, 8, 16
b. 1, 2, 4, 7, 14, 28
c. 1, 2, 5, 10, 25, 50
d. 1, 2, 3, 4, 6, 8, 9, 12, 18, 24, 36, 72

Exercise 6.2.2

a. 6   b. 16   c. 5   d. 9

Exercise 6.3

a. The sum of the digits in $6732 = 18$, and 18 is divisible by 9. Therefore 6732 is divisible by 9. The last two digits of 67<u>32</u> are divisible by 4, therefore 6732 is divisible by 4.
b. 48   c. 24

Exercise 6.4

a. i. 16   ii. 49   iii. 8   iv. 10   v. 7
b. i. 4^4 ii. 6^2
c. 36

Exercise 6.5.1

a. $2^2 \times 3^2$ b. 2×5^2 c. $2^2 \times 31$ d. 3×5^2

Exercise 6.5.2

a. 64   b. 245

Exercise 6.5.3

a. 2 and 224   b. 8 and 168

Chapter 7 – Rates, ratios and proportions

Rates, ratios and proportions are practical applications of mathematics that help us understand and solve many problems that occur in everyday life. They commonly involve values of time, distance, weight and money.

7.1 Rates

A rate is the comparison (or ratio) of two values, such as kilometres per hour. The word 'per' can be understood as the division of two values, where the denominator is a single unit of measurement. Some examples are

$$\textbf{speed} = \frac{\textbf{distance}}{\textbf{time}} \qquad \textbf{average speed} = \frac{\textbf{total distance}}{\textbf{total time}}$$

Graphs are helpful to model rates. The variable on the vertical axis is the numerator and the variable on the horizontal axis is the denominator.

The graph below models a person walking, where the rate is kilometres per minute (km/min).

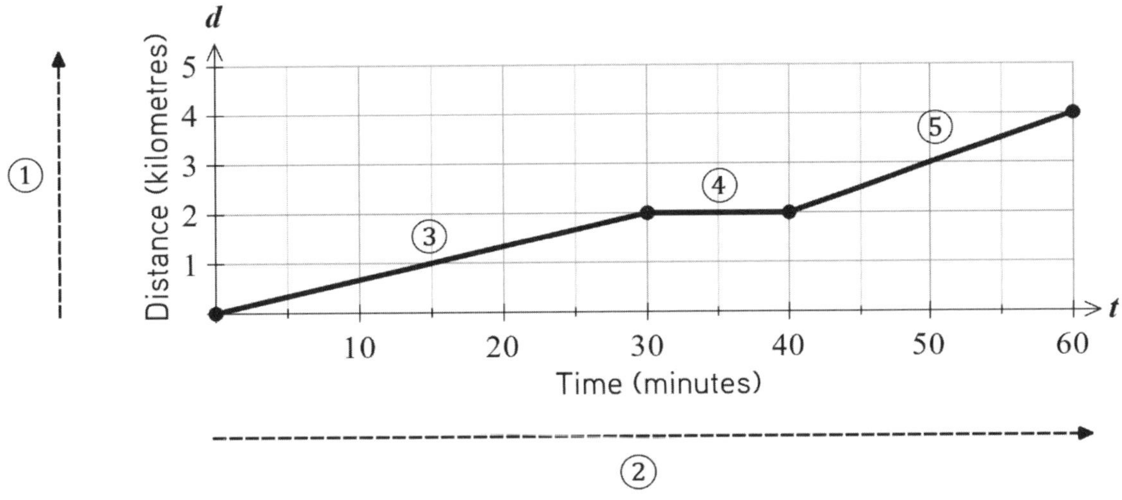

① The vertical scale is the walking distance, in kilometres, which ranges from 0 to 5 ($0 \le d \le 5$).

② The horizontal scale is the time, in minutes, which ranges from 0 to 60 ($0 \le t \le 60$).

③ Using the speed formula shown, we can calculate the walking speed by reading values from the graph.

$$\begin{aligned}\text{speed} &= \frac{2}{30} \\ &= \frac{4\text{ km}}{60\text{ min}} \\ &= 4\text{ km/h}\end{aligned}$$

Often, we need to convert the rate to units that are more commonly used. In the example above we converted minutes to hours, as speed is usually measured in kilometres per hour.

④ A flat section in a distance versus time graph represents time continuing but no distance being covered (the person stopped walking for 10 minutes).

⑤ Steeper sections of the graph indicate an increase in speed.

$$\text{speed} = \frac{2}{20}$$
$$= \frac{6 \text{ km}}{60 \text{ min}}$$
$$= 6 \text{ km/h}$$

Example

The graph below represents income versus time for an employee over the course of an eight-hour shift.

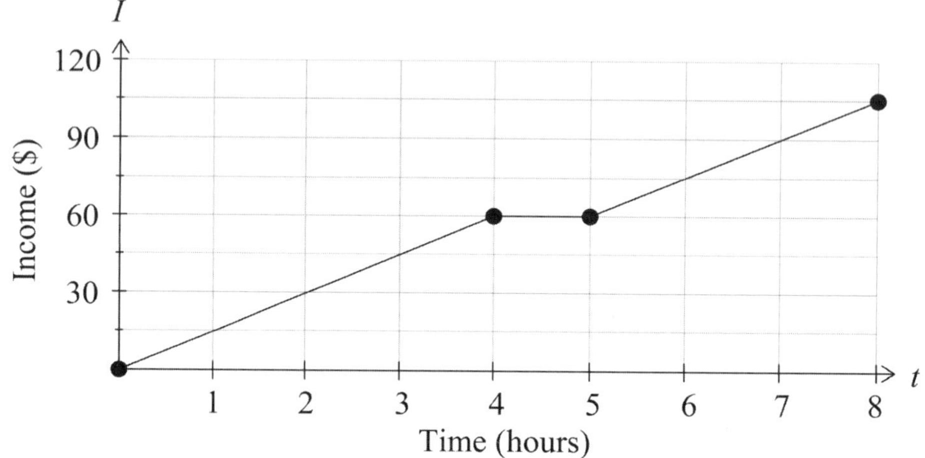

a. How much money did the employee earn in the eight-hour shift?

b. Determine the rate of pay (that is, the hourly wage) paid by the employer.

c. How long was the unpaid lunch break?

d. What is the average hourly wage with the lunch break included?

✓ *Solution*

Working	Explanation
a. $105	Read the value from the vertical axis. The scale on the vertical axis is increasing by $15.
b. $\frac{60}{4} = \$15$ per hour	Select a point that is not within a flat section of the graph and where the required division will be easy.
c. 1 hour	The flat section represents a period where time is continuing but the employee is not being paid (that is, receiving no income).
d. $\frac{105}{8} = \$13.125$	Divide the total income by the total time to find average rate of income.

Exercise 7.1.1

The graph below represents income versus time for an employee over the course of a week.

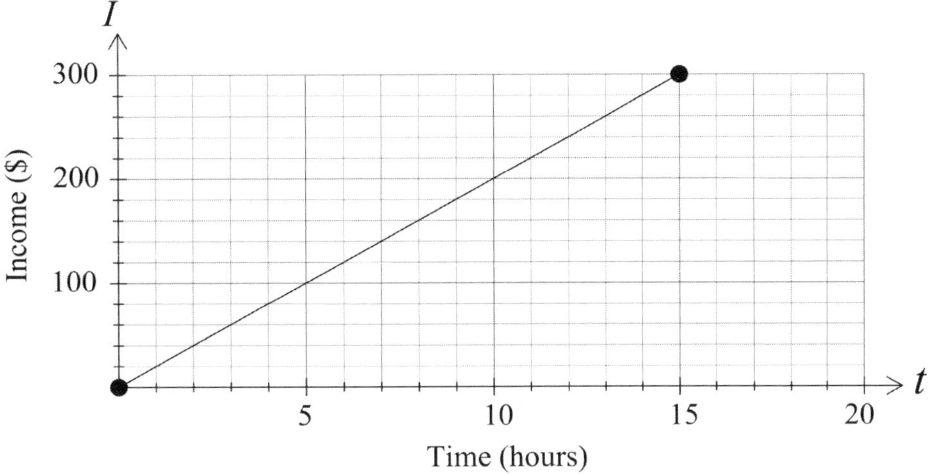

a. How much money did the employee earn in 5 hours?

b. What is the hourly wage of the employee?

c. Determine a rule that connects time (t) and income (I).

d. Use the rule from part **c.** to determine how much money the employee would make after 25 hours of work.

Exercise 7.1.2

The graph below models a person driving a car over a 12-hour period, where the rate is kilometres per hour (km/h).

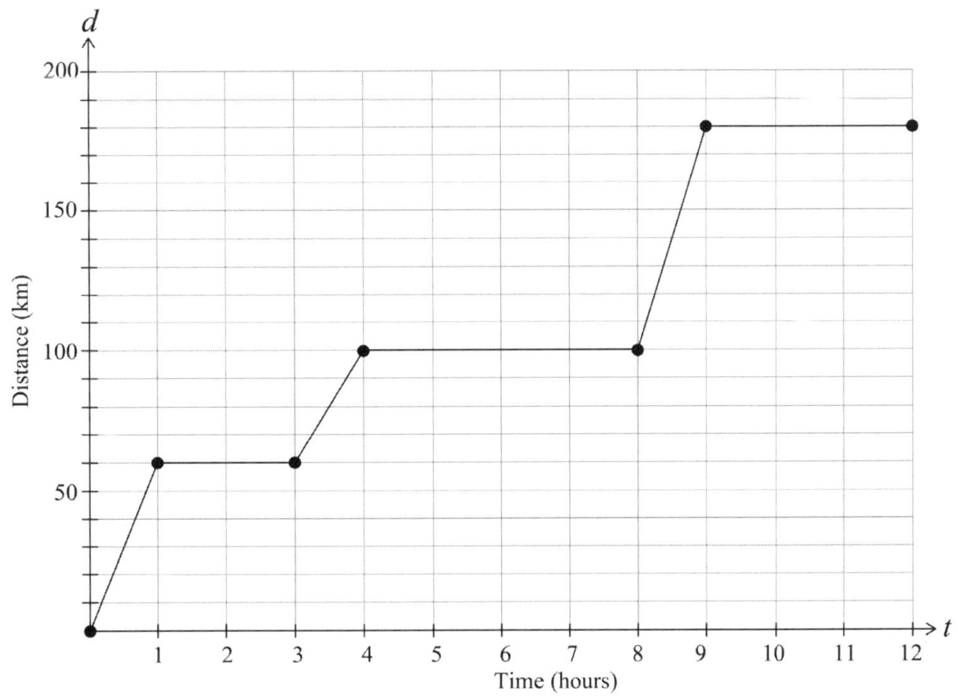

a. How fast was the car going in the first hour?

b. How many kilometres were driven in the 12-hour period?

c. How long in total was the car parked?

d. What was the fastest speed in the 12-hour period?

e. What was the slowest speed in the 12-hour period?

7.2 Ratios

Ratios are used to compare quantities that have the same units. In a ratio ':' is read as 'to'. All quantities must have the same units, and any fractions or decimals in ratios must be simplified to leave the ratio in its simplest form.

Example

In a group of 10 animals there are 4 penguins and 6 seals.

a. Determine the ratio of penguins to seals.

b. Determine the ratio of seals to penguins.

c. Determine the ratio of seals to total animals.

✓ Solution

Working	Explanation
a. $4:6 = 2:3$	The wording of the question determines the order of the ratio. Always write ratios in simplest form.
b. $6:4 = 3:2$	The order is now switched to 'seals to penguins'.
c. $6:10 = 3:5$	Seals to total animals is equivalent to the fraction of seals as a part of the whole.

Example

An art student is making 300 mL of paint from three colours: red, yellow and blue. The colours need to be mixed in the ratio red : yellow : blue $= 2:3:5$.

Determine the quantity needed of each colour.

✓ ***Solution***

Working	Explanation
$2+3+5=10$	Determine the total number of parts in the ratio.
$\frac{300}{10}=30$	Divide the total amount of paint by the total number of parts. This gives the amount of paint per part.
red $= 2 \times 30 = 60$ mL yellow $= 3 \times 30 = 90$ mL blue $= 5 \times 30 = 150$ mL	Multiply each part of the ratio by the amount of paint per part.

Exercise 7.2.1

Divide each of the following dollar amounts into the given ratio.

a. $\$40\ (1:3)$ **b.** $\$75\ (3:2)$ **c.** $\$200\ (9:1)$ **d.** $\$120\ (4:2)$

e. $\$9\ (1:2)$ **f.** $\$1.50\ (1:2)$ **g.** $\$12.60\ (2:7)$ **h.** $\$4.40\ (5:6)$

Exercise 7.2.2

Mortar is being made using sand and cement in the ratio of $5:3$.

a. How many kilograms of sand and cement are required to make 40 kg of mortar?

b. How many kilograms of cement are required if 20 kg of sand is used?

c. How many kilograms of sand are required if 6 kg of cement is used?

Exercise 7.2.3

A blended fruit drink consists of orange, berry and watermelon juice mixed in the ratio $5:2:1$. How many mL of each type of juice are required to make 200 mL of the drink?

7.3 Proportions

When two ratios are equivalent, they are said to be in the same **proportion**.

Algebra is required to solve for the unknown values in proportional ratios when the solution is not initially clear.

Consider the proportional ratio $5:6 = x:18$. The process to determine the value of x is:

$\frac{5}{6}=\frac{x}{18}$	**1.** Convert the ratios to fractions with the unknown variable as one of the numerators.
$\frac{5 \times 18}{6}=x$ $x=15$	**2.** Cross-multiply to solve for x.

Example

The toppings for a pizza include 150 g of cheese and 90 g of sauce.

a. What is the ratio of cheese to sauce?

b. If the cheese and sauce combined make 75% of the pizza, what is the weight in grams of the remaining toppings?

c. If we only have 60 g of sauce to use, how much cheese would we need?

✓ *Solution*

Working	Explanation
a. $150:90 = 5:3$	Find the HCF of 150 and 90 (30) and simplify the ratio.
b. $x:240 = 25:75$	Set up the proportional statement, with the ratio of the weights equalling the percentage ratio.
$\frac{x}{240} = \frac{25}{75}$ $x = \frac{240 \times 1}{3}$ $x = 80$ g	Convert the ratio to fractions with the unknown variable as a numerator. Solve for x.
c. $5:3 = c:60$	Set up the proportional statement, with the simplified ratio of cheese to sauce equalling the ratio of cheese needed to the amount of sauce we have.
$\frac{5}{3} = \frac{c}{60}$ $\frac{5 \times 60}{3} = c$ $c = 100$ g	Convert the ratio to fractions with the unknown variable as a numerator. Solve for c.

Exercise 7.3.1

Determine the value of x that makes the following proportional statements true.

a. $x:10 = 9:5$ b. $6:x = 7:35$ c. $8:28 = x:70$

Exercise 7.3.2

Gardener Jim charged $990 for a landscaping job. A second gardener, Kim, was required to help complete the job in time. Jim worked for a total of 12 hours and Kim worked for a total of 3 hours.

a. How much should each gardener get paid?

b. What percentage of the job did Kim complete?

7.4 Combined applications

In this section we combine a number of the techniques discussed in this chapter.

The following conversion charts may be helpful. It is worth committing these charts to memory (as well as the time conversion charts in Chapter 4), as conversion is a common practice in mathematics.

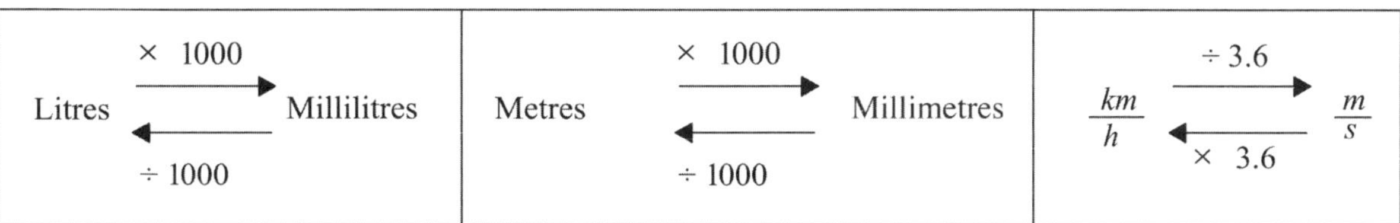

Example

An emu can run 60 m in 4 seconds.

a. How far would it run in 25 seconds at the same speed?

b. How long would it take the emu to run 120 m?

c. How fast is the emu running in kilometres per hour?

✓ Solution

Working	Explanation
a. $\frac{60}{4} = \frac{15}{1} \frac{\text{m}}{\text{sec}}$	Simplify the rate so that the denominator is a single unit.
$15 \times 25 = 375$ m	Multiply the speed by the time to determine the distance.
b. $120 \div 15 = 8$ sec	Divide the distance by the speed (calculated in part **a.**) to derive the time.
c. $15 \times 3.6 = 54 \frac{\text{km}}{\text{h}}$	Use the conversion chart above to convert the speed from m/sec to km/h.

✎ Exercise 7.4.1

The interior angles of a triangle are in the ratio 2 : 3 : 4. Recall that the interior angles of a triangle add up to 180 degrees. Determine the size of each angle.

✎ Exercise 7.4.2

Alex hiked 18 km of a 22.5 km bushwalk in 6 hours.

a. How long will it take Alex to walk the final 4.5 km if the average speed is maintained?

b. If Alex's speed drops to 1.5 km/h for the final 4.5 km, how long would the total walk take?

Exercise 7.4.3

The dose for a certain medicine is 4 mL for every 15 kg of body mass. How much of the medicine should be given to someone who weighs 75 kg?

Exercise 7.4.4

A car can average 300 km on 20 L of fuel.

a. How far would it travel on 50 L of fuel?

b. How many litres of fuel would the car use travelling 480 km?

Exercise 7.4.5

A piece of jewellery is made of gold, platinum and silver in the ratio $2:3:5$. If there are 3 grams of gold in it, how many grams of silver are in it?

Answers

Exercise 7.1.1

a. \$100 b. \$20/h c. $I = 20t$ d. \$500

Exercise 7.1.2

a. 60 km/h b. 180 km c. 9 hours d. 80 km/h

e. 40 km/h

Exercise 7.2.1

a. $10:30$ b. $45:30$ c. $180:20$ d. $80:40$

e. $3:6$ f. $0.50:1$ g. $2.80:9.80$ h. $2:2.40$

Exercise 7.2.2

a. 25 kg of sand and 15 kg of cement b. 12 kg of cement

c. 10 kg of sand

Exercise 7.2.3

125 mL of orange, 50 mL of berry and 25 mL of watermelon

Exercise 7.3.1

a. $x = 18$ b. $x = 30$ c. $x = 20$

Exercise 7.3.2

a. Jim should be paid $792 and Kim should be paid $198.

b. 20%

Exercise 7.4.1

40 degrees, 60 degrees and 80 degrees

Exercise 7.4.2

a. 1.5 hours

b. 9 hours

Exercise 7.4.3

20 mL

Exercise 7.4.4

a. 750 km

b. 32 L

Exercise 7.4.5

7.5 g

Chapter 8 – Algebra

Before we begin working on some mathematical problems, let's refresh our knowledge of the vocabulary (that is, the words) used with algebra.

8.1 Introduction to algebra

Suppose that a student in a maths class uses the letter n to represent the number of lollies in a jar.

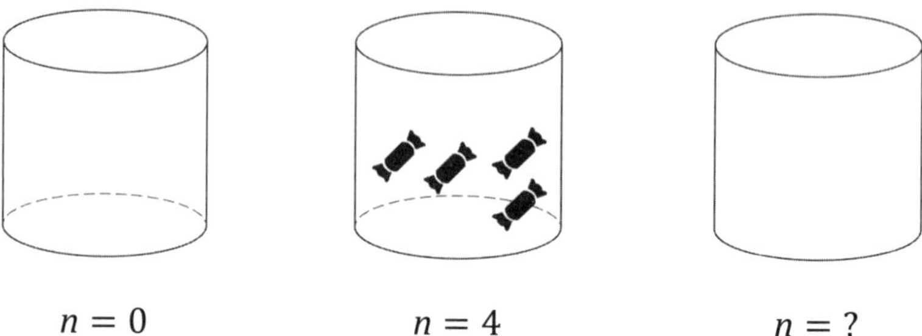

When a letter stands for a number, the letter is called a **pronumeral**.

If we have many jars with different numbers of lollies in them, the value of the pronumeral n could change. In this case it is called a **variable**.

If there are 3 lollies outside the jar and n lollies in the jar, we can write this as an algebraic **expression** that represents the total number of lollies.

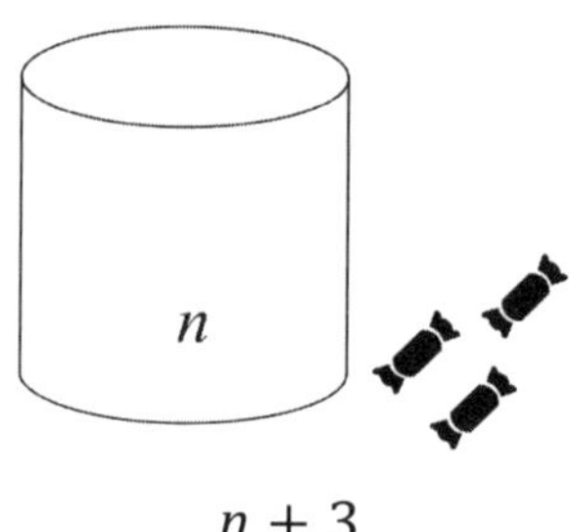

Each part of the expression $n + 3$ is called a **term**, so the expression $n + 3$ has two terms.

If we have two jars of n lollies, we can write the total number of lollies as $n + n$ or $2 \times n$.

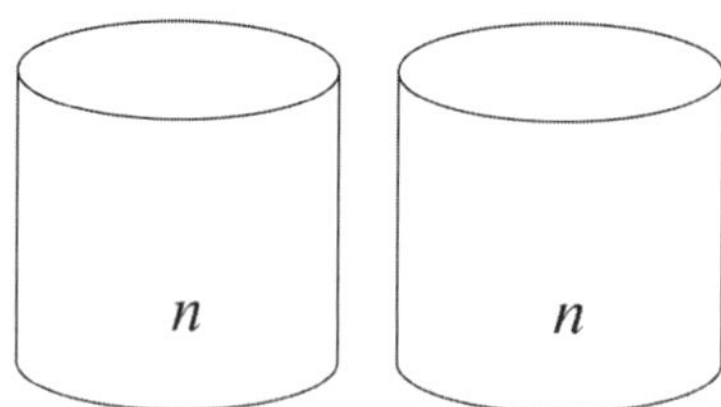

In algebra we do not write the multiplication sign in $2 \times n$. Instead, we write $2n$, where 2 is the **coefficient** of the variable n.

Example

Five jars contain n lollies and there are 4 extra lollies not in the jars.

a. Write an expression for the total number of lollies.

b. Calculate the total number of lollies if $n = 6$.

✓ Solution

Working	Explanation
a. $n + n + n + n + n + 4 = 5n + 4$	Five jars of n lollies can be written many ways. The most efficient way is with a coefficient of 5. The 4 extra lollies are not in the jars, so they are added to the expression as a separate term.
b. $5(6) + 4 = 30 + 4$ $= 34$	We are now told that each jar contains 6 lollies. This means that we can replace the variable n with the value 6. Remember that $5n$ means $5 \times n$. Use brackets instead of a multiplication sign.

Exercise 8.1.1

A student has a pencil case on their desk containing n pencils, and 2 extra pencils beside the case.

a. Write an algebraic expression for the total number of pencils.

b. If 5 more pencils are put on the desk, what is the expression now?

c. If there are 13 pencils in the pencil case, how many are there in total?

Exercise 8.1.2

Write each of the following algebraic expressions in its simplest form.

a. $2 \times a \times a \times a$ **b.** $3 \times x \times 4 \times y$

c. $9 \div x$ **d.** $6 \times x \times 2 \div 4$

Exercise 8.1.3

A rideshare company offers two sizes of transport. One can fit 4 passengers and the other can fit 6. If there are x smaller options and y larger options, write an algebraic expression that represents the total number of passengers that can be transported at the same time.

8.2 Creating algebraic expressions

We can change the order of the terms in an expression as long as we keep the coefficient (and its sign) with the pronumeral. This is illustrated in the following table.

the **sum** of n and 6	$n + 6$	is the same as	$6 + n$
the **difference** between twice x and 1	$2x - 1$	is the same as	$-1 + 2x$
the **product** of m and 3	$m \times 3$	is the same as	$3m$

Example

Translate the following into algebraic expressions, using n to represent the number.

a. Subtract 4 from three times a number.

b. Add 10 to a quarter of a number.

c. The product of 5 and a number halved.

✓ *Solution*

Working	Explanation
a. $3n - 4$	Start from whichever operation is closest to the number n. That operation is **times** (that is, multiply). Read: 'a number' 'times three' 'subtract four' n $\times 3$ -4
b. $\frac{n}{4} + 10$	Read: 'a number', 'quartered' and then 'add 10'.
c. $5\left(\frac{n}{2}\right)$ or $\frac{5n}{2}$	Read: 'a number' 'halved' then 'multiplied by 5' n $\div 2$ $\times 5$ Both expressions shown are correct.

Exercise 8.2

Translate the following into algebraic expressions.

a. the sum of a number (n) and 7

b. the difference between a number (n) and 5 (where 5 is larger than n)

c. the sum of x, y and 14

d. the product of x and 8

e. the quotient when 12 is divided by x

f. x is doubled and then 5 is added

g. y is halved and then 2 is subtracted

h. the product of x and 6 is divided by 12

8.3 Substitution

Replacing a variable in an expression with a number is called **substitution.**

When substituting a number for a variable, it is recommended to use brackets instead of the multiplication symbol, especially when substituting negative values.

Example

The perimeter of a book is two times the width (w) plus two times the length (l).

a. Create an algebraic formula that represents the perimeter (P) of the book.

b. If the width of the book is 21 cm and the length is 30 cm, use the formula from part **a.** to calculate its perimeter.

✓ *Solution*

	Working	Explanation
a.	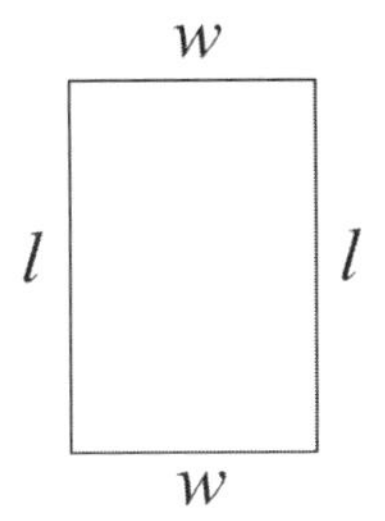 $P = l + w + l + w$ $= 2w + 2l$	Drawing a diagram and labelling the sides can help in seeing what the algebraic formula should be.
b.	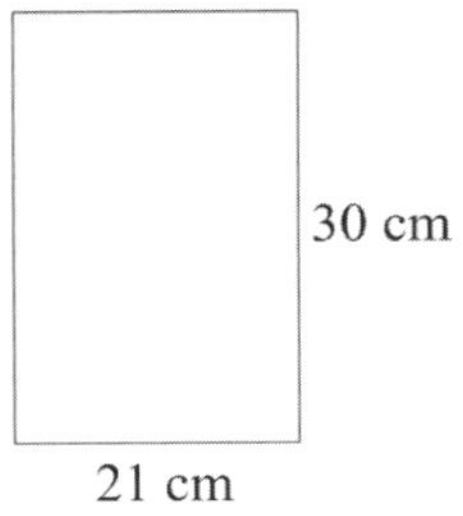 $P = 2w + 2l$ $= 2(21) + 2(30)$ $= 42 + 60$ $= 102$ cm	Substitute the values of the width and length into the formula, using brackets to show multiplication. Write the final answer with appropriate units of measurement.

Exercise 8.3.1

Find the value of each of the following expressions if 8 is substituted for n.

a. $n + 6$ **b.** $15 - n$ **c.** $3n - 4$

d. $34 - 2n$ **e.** $\frac{n}{2} + 1$

Exercise 8.3.2

A regular pentagon has sides of x centimetres.

a. Write an expression that represents the perimeter of the pentagon.

b. If the sides are 3 cm in length, calculate the perimeter of the pentagon.

8.4 Like terms

Like terms are terms in an expression that can be added together or subtracted from each other.

All numbers that are **constants** can be added to or subtracted from each other, but terms with pronumerals are only like terms if the terms share the same letter or letters.

Example

Write $x + x + 3 + 5 + y + y + x$ in a shorter way by combining like terms.

✓ Solution

Working	Explanation
$\underline{x} + \underline{x} + 3 + 5 + \overset{\downarrow}{y} + \overset{\downarrow}{y} + \underline{x}$ $= 3x + 2y + 8$	Mark the pronumerals that are like terms and group them together. The constants 3 and 5 can be added together. **Remember**: only terms with the same pronumeral are like terms.

Example

Write $2xy - 6 + 10 + xy + x$ in a shorter way by combining like terms.

✓ Solution

Working	Explanation
$2\overset{\downarrow}{xy} - 6 + 10 + \overset{\downarrow}{xy} + x$ $= 3xy + x + 4$	Mark the pronumerals that are like terms and group them together. **Note:** $3xy$ and x are not like terms.

Example

Write $9n + n^2 - n + 1$ in a shorter way by combining like terms.

✓ Solution

Working	Explanation
$9\overset{\downarrow}{n} + n^2 - \overset{\downarrow}{n} + 1$ $= n^2 + 8n + 1$	Mark the pronumerals that are like terms and group them together. **Note:** n and n^2 are not like terms.

Exercise 8.4

Simplify the following algebraic expressions.

a. $5x + 2x + 3x + x$

b. $10y - 3y + 2x + 4x$

c. $3x - 4y + 10x + 5y$

d. $5x^2 - 2x^2 + xy + 3xy$

e. $4ab + 3a + 4b + 5ba$

f. $4x + 2y - 6 - 2y$

8.5 Expanding

Brackets are used in algebra in a similar way to how they are used with numbers. We can think of them as repeated addition. For example, $3(x + 2)$ is the same as 3 lots of $x + 2$.

$$\begin{aligned} 3(x+2) &= x + 2 + x + 2 + x + 2 \\ &= 3x + 6 \end{aligned}$$

As we become better at multiplying, it is more efficient to **expand** brackets.

Example

Consider the expression $2(x + 5)$.

a. Represent the expression with a diagram.

b. Write $2(x + 5)$ without brackets.

c. Evaluate the expression when $x = 8$.

✓ Solution

Working	Explanation
a. 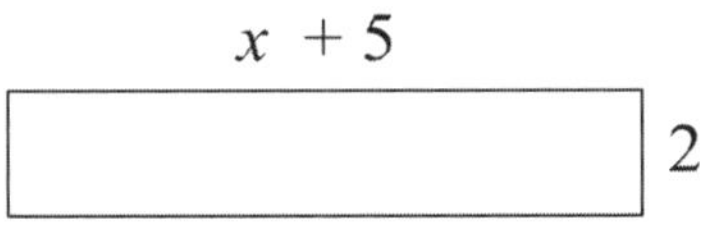	We are multiplying 2 by both terms in the brackets. We can use a rectangle with one term as the width and the other term as the length. Expanding the expression is then like finding the area of the rectangle.
b. $2x + 10$	Multiply each term inside the brackets by the term outside the brackets.
c. $2(8) + 10 = 16 + 10$ $= 26$	Substitute $x = 8$ into the expression from part **b.** and evaluate it.

Exercise 8.5.1

Show that when $x = 4$ is substituted into both the expanded and non-expanded form of $4(x + 6)$ the solutions are equal.

Exercise 8.5.2

Expand the following expressions, collecting like terms where appropriate.

a. $3(x + 5)$
b. $6(x - 4)$
c. $7(x + 1) + 9$
d. $6(x - 3) + 4(x + 5)$
e. $-2(x - 3)$
f. $-(x + 1)$

8.6 Applications of algebra

Algebra can help us solve mathematical problems that seem very complicated at first, but by using the skills covered in this chapter we can make them easier to understand.

We will sometimes need to draw on our knowledge of measurement and geometry in solving algebraic problems.

Example

A rectangular desk is three times as long as it is wide.

a. Write an algebraic expression for the perimeter of the desk in terms of the variable x.
b. Write an algebraic expression for the area of the desk in terms of the variable x.
c. If $x = 30$ cm, calculate the perimeter and area of the desk.

✓ Solution

Working	Explanation
a. 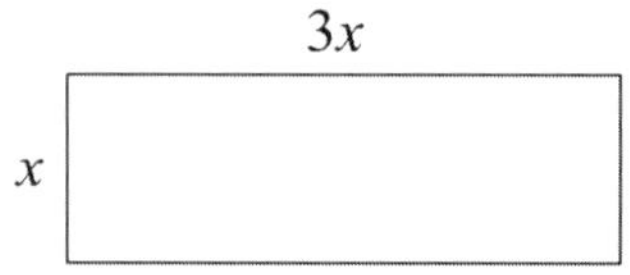	It will help if you draw a rectangle and label the sides with the variable stated in the question.
$P = 3x + x + 3x + x$ $= 8x$	The perimeter is the sum of all the side lengths.
b. $A = 3x \times x$ $= 3x^2$	The area of a rectangle is length × width.
c. $P = 8(30)$ $= 240$ cm $A = 3(30)^2$ $= 3(900)$ $= 2700$ cm^2	Substitute $x = 30$ into each equation. Always add the appropriate unit of measurement.

Exercise 8.6.1

An equilateral triangle has sides of length x cm.

a. Write an algebraic expression for the perimeter.

b. Calculate the perimeter when $x = 6$ cm.

Exercise 8.6.2

An odd number, n, is added to the next consecutive odd number, $n + 2$.

a. Write an algebraic expression that is the sum of four consecutive odd numbers.

b. Using your answer from part **a.** calculate the sum of four consecutive odd numbers if the starting number is 7.

Exercise 8.6.3

A rectangle has side lengths (in centimetres) of $n + 5$ and 12.

a. Write an algebraic expression for the perimeter of the rectangle.

b. If the rectangle doubles in both length and width, what would be the new perimeter?

Answers

Exercise 8.1.1

a. $n + 2$ **b.** $n + 7$ **c.** 20

Exercise 8.1.2

a. $2a^3$ **b.** $12xy$ **c.** $\frac{9}{x}$ **d.** $3x$

Exercise 8.1.3

$4x + 6y$

Exercise 8.2

a. $n + 7$ **b.** $5 - n$ **c.** $x + y + 14$ **d.** $8x$

e. $\frac{12}{x}$ **f.** $2x + 5$ **g.** $\frac{y}{2} - 2$ **h.** $\frac{x}{2}$

Exercise 8.3.1

a. 14 **b.** 7 **c.** 20 **d.** 18

e. 5

Exercise 8.3.2

a. $5x$ **b.** 15 cm

Exercise 8.4

a. $11x$
b. $7y + 6x$
c. $13x + y$
d. $3x^2 + 4xy$
e. $9ab + 3a + 4b$
f. $4x - 6$

Exercise 8.5.1

$4(x + 6)$
$= 4x + 24$

$4(4 + 6)$
$= 4(10)$
$= 40$

$4(4) + 24$
$= 16 + 24$
$= 40$

Exercise 8.5.2

a. $3x + 15$
b. $6x - 24$
c. $7x + 16$
d. $10x + 2$
e. $-2x + 6$
f. $-x - 1$

Exercise 8.6.1

a. $3x$
b. 18 cm

Exercise 8.6.2

a. $4n + 12$
b. 40

Exercise 8.6.3

a. $2n + 34$
b. $4n + 68$

Chapter 9 – Solving equations

9.1 Introduction to equations

An algebraic equation is two expressions on either side of an equals (=) sign.

The equals sign means that the left side and the right side are **equivalent**.

Equations can be written in many forms. We could, for example, use boxes to represent the unknown number in an equation, or we could use pronumerals.

Example

Find the missing value to make the following equation true.

$$10 \times \square - 4 = 26$$

✓ *Solution*

Working	Explanation
$10 \times 3 - 4 = 26$	We need to find the missing number that will make the left-hand side of the equation equal to 26. If we choose 2 as the missing number, the equation becomes $10 \times 2 - 4 = 16$. This is not 26, so 2 is not the correct answer.
$x = 3$	By trial and error we will find that the left-hand side of the equation is equal to the right-hand side only if the missing number is 3. We say that $x = 3$ is the **solution** to this equation.

Example

Find the value of the pronumeral that makes the equation $2x + 6 = 14$ true.

✓ *Solution*

Working	Explanation
$2 \times 4 + 6 = 14$	If we choose 3 as the missing number, the equation becomes $2 \times 3 + 6 = 12$ (not 14).
$x = 4$	By trial and error we will find that the left-hand side of the equation is equal to the right-hand side only if the missing number is 4. Therefore $x = 4$ is the solution to this equation.

Exercise 9.1

Solve each of the following equations by finding the value of the pronumeral that makes the equation true.

a. $6x = 18$ b. $20 - y = 14$ c. $m + 12 = 30$

d. $x + 4 = 0$ e. $2y + 1 = 11$ f. $3(t - 2) = 27$

9.2 Equivalent equations

There are other ways of solving an equation than by guessing a value and checking to see if it makes the equation true. It will help if we think of an equation as a set of scales that we keep in balance (that is, with each side equal to the other).

Suppose that we want to solve the equation $x + 2 = 5$.

Imagine that x represents the mass of an object, say a duck, and any unit value is represented by ❶.

We can represent this equation with a set of scales.

$$x + 2 = 5$$

Notice that the scales are in balance, because the sides are equal.

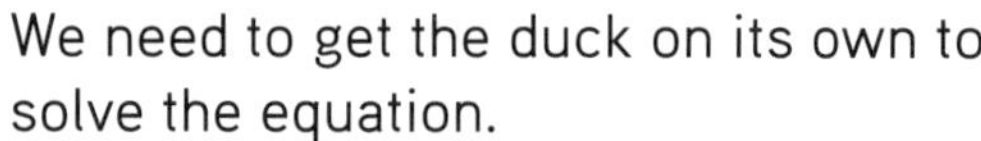

We need to get the duck on its own to solve the equation.

So we remove (subtract) the two weights from the left side.

But for the scales to remain balanced, we must also remove two weights from the right side.

$$x + 2 - 2 = 5 - 2$$

$$x + 0 = 3$$

When we simplify the equation, we find that $x = 3$.

So $x = 3$ is equivalent to the equation $x + 2 = 5$.

Example

Without drawing scales, determine the simpler equivalent equation to each of the following equations.

a. $x + 7 = 23$ b. $6 + x = 10$ c. $x - 8 = 19$ d. $x - 11 = 3$

✓ *Solution*

Working	Explanation
a. $x + \not{7} = 23 - 7$ $x = 16$	Subtract 7 from the left side to get x on its own. However, we must also subtract 7 from the right side to maintain a balanced equation.
b. $\not{6} + x = 10 - 6$ $x = 4$	Subtract 6 from the left side to get x on its own. However, we must also subtract 6 from the right side to maintain a balanced equation.
c. $x - \not{8} = 19 + 8$ $x = 27$	Add 8 to the left side to get x on its own. Therefore we must add 8 to the right to maintain a balanced equation.
d. $x - \not{11} = 3 + 11$ $x = 14$	Add 11 to the left side to get x on its own, and add 11 to the right to maintain a balanced equation.

Exercise 9.2

Solve each of the following equations for the unknown pronumeral. You may want to draw a balance scale to help.

a. $23 = 10 + x$ **b.** $5 + 2x = 19$ **c.** $10 = 2y + 4$

d. $7a + 2 = 44$ **e.** $3 = 2b - 15$ **f.** $34 + 2x = 4x + 14$

g. $y + 6 = 3y + 2$ **h.** $2(x + 4) = 10 + x$

9.3 Solving equations algebraically

We are now going to solve equations algebraically. To repeat: the solution to an equation is a number that we can substitute for a variable so that the equation will be true. We can check if a potential solution is correct by substituting it into the original equation.

Example

Solve the equation $2x + 6 = 22$.

✓ *Solution*

Working	Explanation
$2x + 6 = 22$ $2x + \not{6} - \not{6} = 22 - 6$ $2x = 16$ $\frac{\not{2}x}{\not{2}} = \frac{16}{2}$ $x = 8$	Subtract 6 from both sides of the equation. Divide both sides by 2. State the solution.
$2(8) + 6 = 16 + 6$ $= 22$	Check the answer by substituting the solution into the original equation and looking to see if the equation is true.

Example

Solve the equation $9 = 2x - 4$.

✓ ***Solution***

Working	Explanation
$9 = 2x - 4$ $9 + 4 = 2x - \cancel{4} + \cancel{4}$ $13 = 2x$ $\frac{13}{2} = \frac{\cancel{2}x}{\cancel{2}}$ $x = \frac{13}{2}$	Add 4 to both sides of the equation. Divide both sides by 2. State the solution.
$2\left(\frac{13}{2}\right) - 4 = \cancel{2}\left(\frac{13}{\cancel{2}}\right) - 4$ $= 13 - 4$ $= 9$	Check the answer by substituting the solution into the original equation and looking to see if the equation is true.

Example

Solve the equation $4x - 1 = 2x + 9$.

✓ ***Solution***

Working	Explanation
$4x - 1 = 2x + 9$ $4x - \cancel{1} + \cancel{1} = 2x + 9 + 1$ $4x = 2x + 10$ $4x - 2x = \cancel{2x} - \cancel{2x} + 10$ $2x = 10$ $\frac{\cancel{2}x}{\cancel{2}} = \frac{10}{2}$ $x = 5$	Add 1 to both sides of the equation. Subtract $2x$ from both sides of the equation. Divide both sides by 2. State the solution.
LHS $= 4(5) - 1$ RHS $= 2(5) + 9$ $= 20 - 1$ $= 10 + 9$ $= 19$ $= 19$	Check the answer by substituting the solution into the original equation and looking to see if both sides of the equation are equal.

Exercise 9.3

Solve each of the following equations for x.

a. $3x - 12 = 3$ **b.** $2(x + 4) = 24$ **c.** $3x - 5 = 4$ **d.** $6x + 7 = 25$

e. $-8x = 16$ **f.** $3(x - 2) = 12$ **g.** $6x - 3 = 2x + 9$ **h.** $9x + 1 = 21 - x$

9.4 Formulating equations

The process of creating an algebraic equation to represent a situation is called **formulating** an equation.

Example

A number is doubled and one is added to the result to give 23. Find the number.

✓ *Solution*

Working	Explanation
$2n + 1 = 23$ $2n + \cancel{1} - \cancel{1} = 23 - 1$ $2n = 22$ $\frac{\cancel{2}n}{\cancel{2}} = \frac{22}{2}$ $n = 11$	Select a pronumeral to represent the original number (for example, n). Add 2 as a coefficient to show that we are doubling the number. Add 1. Equate the expression to 23. Solve the equation.

Example

A rectangular paddock has a width of 13 m and an area of 104 m^2. Find the length of the paddock.

✓ *Solution*

Working	Explanation
13 m 104 m^2 l $A = l \times w$ $104 = 13l$ $\frac{104}{13} = \frac{\cancel{13}l}{\cancel{13}}$ $l = 8$ m	Draw a diagram and label it with the given information. Formulate an equation based on our knowledge that the area of a rectangle equals its length multiplied by its width. Substitute the given values. Rearrange the equation to make the pronumeral for length (l) the subject. Solve for l.

Example

The sum of two consecutive odd numbers is 28. Find the numbers.

✓ ***Solution***

Working	Explanation
$n + n + 2 = 28$ $2n + 2 = 28$ $2n + \cancel{2} - \cancel{2} = 28 - 2$ $2n = 26$ $\frac{\cancel{2}n}{\cancel{2}} = \frac{26}{2}$ $n = 13$	'Sum' means addition. 'Consecutive' means in order. Two consecutive odd numbers could be 7, 9 or 27, 29 etc. Use a pronumeral (for example, n) to represent the first odd number in the sequence. The next odd number after n will have a value of $n + 2$. Now we can formulate the equation and solve for n.

Exercise 9.4

Formulate and solve an algebraic equation for each of the following.

a. The sum of 5 and a number, n, is 17. Find n.

b. The sum of three times a number, n, and 6 is 18. Find n.

c. A square has an area of 64 cm^2. Determine the length of its sides.

d. A rectangular box has a volume of 120 cm^3, a width of 5 cm and a height of 6 cm. Determine the length.

e. The sum of two consecutive whole numbers is 35. Find the numbers.

f. The mean (average) of three numbers is 7. If 8 and 11 are two of the numbers, find the third number.

9.5 Applications of equations

The technique of formulating and solving algebraic equations has many useful applications in real life.

Sometimes a diagram or graph can help in understanding a problem before formulating an equation. Also, there may be occasions when we need to convert units before formulating an equation.

Example

Suppose you purchase three movie tickets (for yourself and two friends) and a $7 bucket of popcorn for a total of $40. How much was one ticket?

✓ *Solution*

Working	Explanation
$3n + 7 = 40$ $3n + \cancel{7} - \cancel{7} = 40 - 7$ $3n = 33$ $\frac{\cancel{3}n}{\cancel{3}} = \frac{33}{3}$ $n = 11$ The tickets cost $11 each.	Use a pronumeral (for example, *n*) to represent the cost of one ticket. Formulate the equation, remembering that 3 is the coefficient of n. The cost of popcorn will be in addition to the ticket prices. Solve the equation.

Example

The length of a rectangular garden is two times its width. If the perimeter is 48 m, calculate the dimensions of the garden.

✓ *Solution*

Working	Explanation
$P = w + 2w + w + 2w$ $48 = 6w$ $\frac{48}{6} = \frac{\cancel{6}w}{\cancel{6}}$ $w = 8$ The width is 8 m and the length is 16 m.	Draw a diagram. $2w$ $P = 48 \text{ m}$ w We only need one variable, w, as the length and the width are proportionally related. Formulate an equation for the perimeter of the rectangle. Solve for w.

Exercise 9.5

Use the various techniques discussed earlier in this chapter to formulate equations to solve the following problems.

- **a.** Alex has \$50 to spend. After purchasing two T-shirts, only \$3.20 remains. How much was each T-shirt?
- **b.** The length of a rectangular garden is three times its width. If the perimeter of the garden is 120 m, calculate the dimensions of the garden.
- **c.** A company hires out electrical tools for home maintenance. The company charges a one-off hire fee of \$20 plus a rate of \$150 per day. How much would a 3-day hire cost?
- **d.** Two families leave from the same destination to drive to a holiday resort 240 km away. They each take a different route. One family takes Route 1 and averages 80 km/h. The other family rakes Route 2 and averages 60 km/h. How much quicker was Route 1?
- **e.** A mother is four times older than her daughter. If the sum of their ages is 55, how old are they?

Answers

Exercise 9.1

a. $x = 3$ **b.** $y = 6$ **c.** $m = 18$

d. $x = -4$ **e.** $y = 5$ **f.** $t = 11$

Exercise 9.2

a. $x = 13$ **b.** $x = 7$ **c.** $y = 3$ **d.** $a = 6$

e. $b = 9$ **f.** $x = 10$ **g.** $y = 2$ **h.** $x = 2$

Exercise 9.3

a. $x = 5$ **b.** $x = 8$ **c.** $x = 3$ **d.** $x = 3$

e. $x = -2$ **f.** $x = 6$ **g.** $x = 3$ **h.** $x = 2$

Exercise 9.4

a. $n = 12$ **b.** $n = 4$ **c.** $l = 8$ cm

d. $l = 4$ cm **e.** 17, 18 **f.** 2

Exercise 9.5

a. \$23.40 **b.** $w = 15$ m, $l = 45$ m **c.** \$470

d. 1 hour **e.** 11 and 44

Chapter 10 – Patterns, rules, tables and graphs

We can sometimes solve mathematical problems by observing patterns. Often formulas can be derived from patterns and then used to solve problems more efficiently than by simple repetitive counting techniques.

10.1 Number patterns

Number patterns are also known as mathematical **sequences**. Each number in a sequence is called a **term**. For example, the following sequence has 5 terms.

$$\underbrace{3, 5, 7, 9, 11}_{\text{Sequence}} \qquad \underset{\text{Term Position}}{t_1 = 3}$$

In the sequence above, 3 is the first term. We denote its position by writing t_1. The second term in the sequence is 5. Its position is denoted by t_2. Likewise for the other terms.

To identify a number pattern in a sequence, we look for a **common difference**, that is, we inspect the sequence for consecutive terms that go up or down by the same amount. In the example below the common difference is +2.

$$3 \xrightarrow[+2]{} 5 \xrightarrow[+2]{} 7 \xrightarrow[+2]{} 9 \xrightarrow[+2]{} 11$$

Some number patterns involve a **common ratio**, that is, a term is being multiplied or divided by the same amount each time. The common ratio in the example below is $\times\frac{1}{3}$.

$$189 \xrightarrow[\times\frac{1}{3}]{} 63 \xrightarrow[\times\frac{1}{3}]{} 21 \xrightarrow[\times\frac{1}{3}]{} 7$$

Example

Find the next 3 terms in each of the following sequences.

a. 5, 12, 19, 26, ... **b.** 9, 18, 36, 72, ... **c.** 43, 40, 37, 34, ...

✓ Solution

Working	Explanation
a. 5, 12, 19, 26, $\underline{33}$, $\underline{40}$, $\underline{47}$	The common difference between the terms is +7.
b. 9, 18, 36, 72, $\underline{144}$, $\underline{288}$, $\underline{576}$	The common ratio between the terms is ×2.
c. 43, 40, 37, 34, $\underline{31}$, $\underline{28}$, $\underline{25}$	The common difference between the terms is −3.

Exercise 10.1

Find the next three terms in each of the following number sequences.

a. 2, 4, 8, 16, ___, ___, ___

b. 1, 6, 11, 16, ___, ___, ___

c. 24, 21, 18, 15, ___, ___, ___

d. 160, 80, 40, ___, ___, ___

e. 1, 3, 9, 27, ___, ___, ___

f. 6, 12, 18, 24, ___, ___, ___

10.2 Spatial patterns

Spatial patterns are sequences that involve geometric shapes. We look at features of the shapes and describe them as a number sequence to find the mathematical rule that describes how each shape is connected.

In the example below the number of matchsticks in each spatial pattern determines the value of each term in the corresponding number sequence.

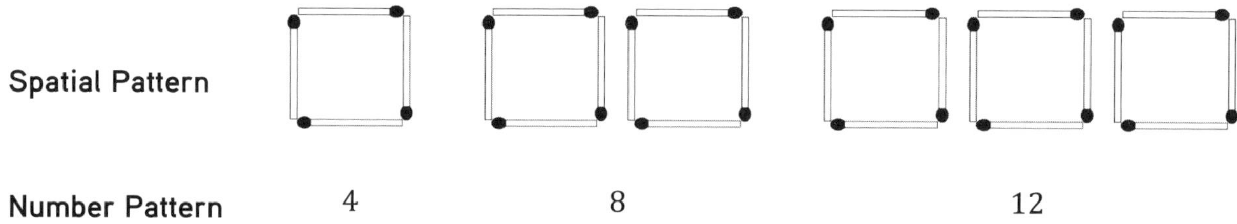

We can describe the pattern as '4 matchsticks initially, requiring 4 additional sticks to make the next term'.

We can describe the pattern in a table.

Number of squares	1	2	3
Number of matchsticks required	4	8	12

Example

Consider the diagram below.

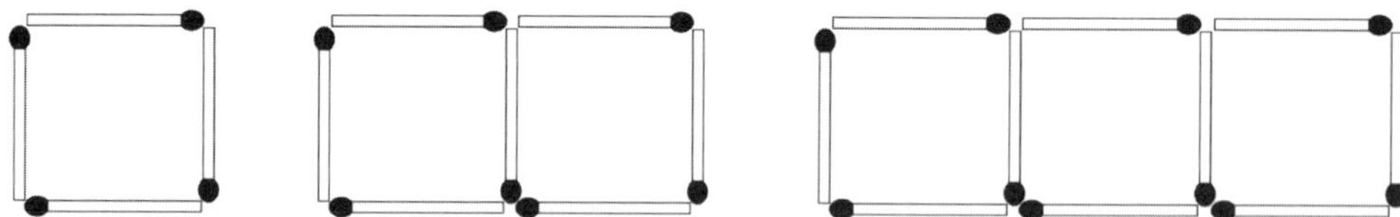

a. Draw the next two shapes in the sequence.

b. Write the spatial pattern as a number sequence and determine the values of terms four and five.

c. Create a table that shows the number of matchsticks required for each shape in the pattern.

d. Determine a rule that connects the number of matchsticks (S) to the number of squares (n) in each spatial pattern.

e. Use the rule from part **d.** to determine how many matchsticks will be required to make 30 squares.

✓ *Solution*

<table>
<tr><th>Working</th><th>Explanation</th></tr>
<tr><td>a.</td><td>Counting the number of matchsticks in each term helps identify the number required for the next shape.</td></tr>
<tr><td>b. $4 \xrightarrow{+3} 7 \xrightarrow{+3} 10 \xrightarrow{+3} 13 \xrightarrow{+3} 16$</td><td>Write the number of matchsticks in each shape as a number sequence and calculate the difference between consecutive terms.</td></tr>
<tr><td>c.
<table>
<tr><td>Number of squares (n)</td><td>1</td><td>2</td><td>3</td><td>4</td><td>5</td></tr>
<tr><td>Number of sticks (S)</td><td>4</td><td>7</td><td>10</td><td>13</td><td>16</td></tr>
</table></td><td>Transfer the number sequence to a table of values.</td></tr>
<tr><td>d.
<table>
<tr><td>Number of squares (n)</td><td>1</td><td>2</td><td>3</td><td>4</td><td>5</td></tr>
<tr><td>Number of sticks (S)</td><td>4</td><td>7</td><td>10</td><td>13</td><td>16</td></tr>
</table>
$d = +3$</td><td>Select any column from part c. (Here we have selected the second column.)</td></tr>
<tr><td>$+3 \times \boxed{2} = 6$</td><td>Multiply the value of the common difference (d) by the number of squares (n).</td></tr>
<tr><td>$6 + ? = \boxed{7}$</td><td>Add or subtract the amount needed to equal the number of matchsticks (S).</td></tr>
<tr><td>$S = d \times n + ?$
$S = 3n + 1$</td><td>This will enable us to find the rule that links number of matchsticks to number of squares.</td></tr>
<tr><td>e. $S = 3n + 1$
$= 3(30) + 1$
$= 91$</td><td>Substitute $n = 30$ into the equation found in part d.</td></tr>
</table>

Exercise 10.2.1

Consider the spatial pattern below and answer the following questions.

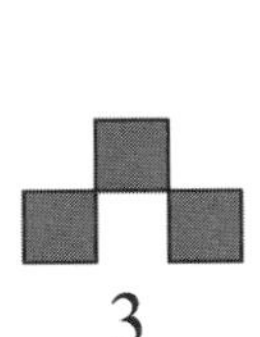

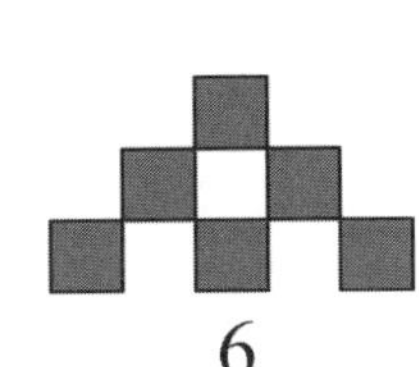

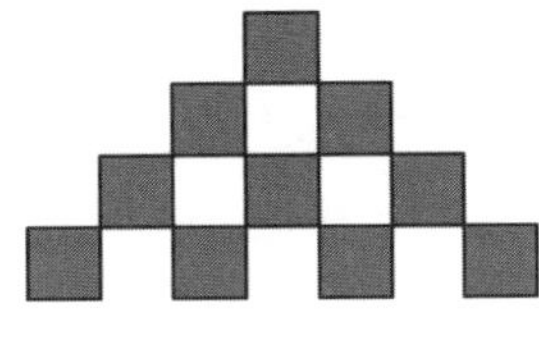

a. Complete the table below.

Pattern number (n)	1	2	3	4	5
Number of squares (S)	3	6	?	?	?

b. Determine the number of squares required for patterns 6 and 7.

Exercise 10.2.2

Consider the spatial pattern below and answer the following questions.

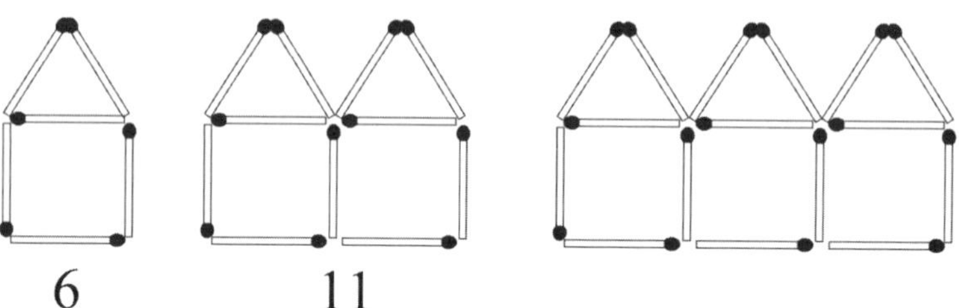

a. Complete the table below.

Pattern number (n)	1	2	3	4	5
Number of matchsticks (S)	6	11	?	?	?

b. Determine the rule that connects the number of matchsticks (S) to the pattern number (n).

c. Use the rule found in part **b.** to determine the number of matchsticks required for pattern number 9.

10.3 Rules and tables

If there is no spatial pattern, a table of values can be created from a rule. The **input** is the values that we put into the rule and the **output** is the numbers that are produced as a result.

If we are filling in a table of values from a rule, substitute each input value into the rule to find the corresponding output value. For example, if the rule is **output** $=$ **2** $\times$ **input** $-$ **3**, we would fill in the table as follows.

Input	0	1	2	3	4
Output	-3	-1	1	3	5

If we are trying to find the rule from a table of values, we find:

1. the product of the common difference (d) and an input value, and
2. determine the value to be added or subtracted to find the output value.

$$\textbf{output} = d \times \textbf{input} \pm ?$$

We call the set of input values the **domain** and the set of output values the **range**.

We use $\{\}$ to list the numbers as a set, separated by commas. For example: $\{0, 1, 2, 3, 4\}$.

Example

Consider the following table of values.

Input	1	2	3	4	5	6
Output	4	7	10	13	?	?

a. Identify the common difference and complete the table.

b. Determine the rule that connects the input and output.

c. State the domain and range.

d. Use the rule found in part **b.** to determine the output when the input is 10.

e. Use the rule found in part **b.** to determine the input when the output is 25.

✓ Solution

<table>
<tr><th>Working</th><th>Explanation</th></tr>
<tr><td>a.
<table><tr><td>Input</td><td>1</td><td>2</td><td>3</td><td>4</td><td>5</td><td>6</td></tr><tr><td>Output</td><td>4</td><td>7</td><td>10</td><td>13</td><td>16</td><td>19</td></tr></table>
$d = 3$</td><td>The common difference (d) is the regular change in the output values. For example, $7 - 4 = 3$, $10 - 7 = 3$ and so on. So $d = 3$.
Use this value to complete the table.</td></tr>
<tr><td>b.
<table><tr><td>Input</td><td>1</td><td>2</td><td>3</td><td>4</td><td>5</td><td>6</td></tr><tr><td>Output</td><td>4</td><td>7</td><td>10</td><td>13</td><td>16</td><td>19</td></tr></table>
output = input $\times 3 + 1$</td><td>Select any input–output column.
Multiply the input value by the common difference: 3×1 if we choose the first input–output column.
From the value obtained, add or subtract the number required to make the calculation equal the output value (4). In this example the number is 1.</td></tr>
<tr><td>c. domain: $\{1, 2, 3, 4, 5, 6\}$
range: $\{4, 7, 10, 13, 16, 19\}$</td><td>The domain is the set of all input values.
The range is the set of all output values.</td></tr>
<tr><td>d. output = input $\times 3 + 1$
$= 10 \times 3 + 1$
$= 31$</td><td>Substitute an input value of 10 into the rule and evaluate the equation.</td></tr>
<tr><td>e. output = input $\times 3 + 1$
25 = input $\times 3 + 1$
input $= 8$</td><td>Substitute 25 into the rule as the output value and solve the equation algebraically, or by asking 'what number, when multiplied by 3 and having 1 added to the result, equals 25?'</td></tr>
</table>

Exercise 10.3.1

Consider the following table of values.

Input	1	2	3	4	5	6
Output	2	6	10	14	18	22

a. Determine the rule that connects the input and output.

b. State the domain and range.

c. Use the rule found in part **a.** to determine the output when the input is 10.

Exercise 10.3.2

Consider the following table of values.

Input	1	2	3	4	5	6
Output	−1	1	3	5	7	9

a. Determine the rule that connects the input and output.

b. State the domain and range.

c. Use the rule found in part **a.** to determine the output when the input is 20.

10.4 Cartesian coordinates

The **Cartesian plane** is a way of representing points by their distance from two number lines:

- a horizontal number line called the ***x*-axis** and
- a vertical number line called the ***y*-axis**.

The axes intersect at what is called the **origin**.

A **coordinate (ordered pair)** is a point on the Cartesian plane that has a horizontal component (the x-coordinate) and vertical component (the y-coordinate). These components can be considered as distances from the origin.

For example, the coordinate $(1, 2)$ is plotted on the following Cartesian plane. It is labelled in the order (x, y).

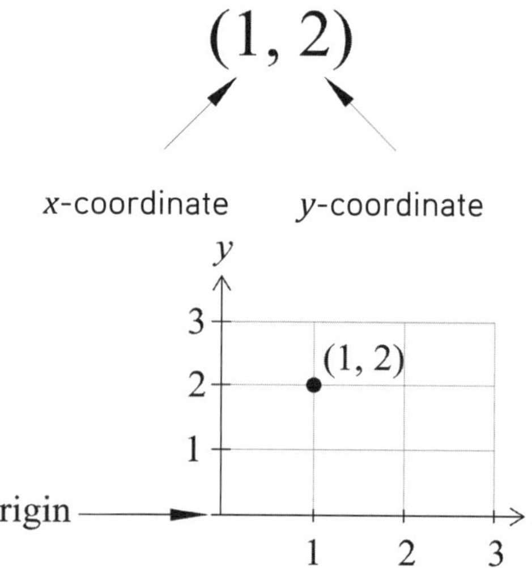

Given a rule, we can fill in a table of values and plot the values as coordinates on the Cartesian plane. An example is shown below.

Input (x)	**Output (y)**
0	1
1	2
2	3
3	4
4	5

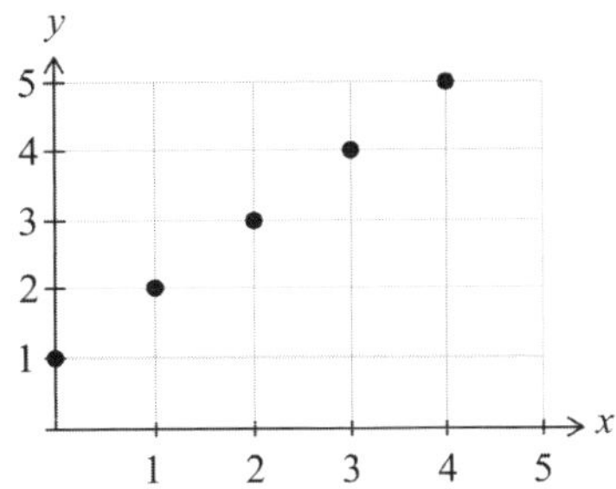

If the coordinates can be connected to form a straight line, as in the example above, the input and output values are in a **linear** relationship. The rule that describes this particular relationship is: 'each y-value is equal to the x-value plus 1'.

If the coordinates cannot be connected to form a straight line, any relationship between the input and output values is a **non-linear** relationship.

Example

A recipe for baking a particular biscuit requires sugar and flour. Let x represent the amount of sugar (in cups), and y represent the amount of flour (also in cups).

Sugar (x)	1	$1\frac{1}{2}$	2	$2\frac{1}{2}$	3	$3\frac{1}{2}$
Flour (y)	2	3	4	5	6	7

a. Represent the amounts of sugar and flour as ordered pairs.

b. Plot the ordered pairs as points on the Cartesian plane.

c. Given that the amount of flour is always twice the amount of sugar, write a rule that connects y and x.

d. How much flour would be required if 6 cups of sugar are used?

✓ Solution

Working	Explanation
a. $(1, 2), \left(1\frac{1}{2}, 3\right), (2, 4), \left(2\frac{1}{2}, 5\right), (3, 6), \left(3\frac{1}{2}, 7\right)$	Always write the pairs in the order (x, y).
b.	Always look at the scale when a set of axes is provided, or create an appropriate scale when making your own set of axes. The scale needs to be sufficient so that both the domain and range can be represented.
c. $y = 2x$	Write a rule in the form $y =$ _______
d. $y = 2(6)$ $= 12$	Substitute $x = 6$ into the rule from part **c**.

Exercise 10.4.1

Consider the rule **output** = **input** − 2.

a. Complete the table of values shown at the right.

b. Write each pair of inputs and outputs from the table as a set of coordinates.

c. Plot each set of coordinates on the Cartesian plane.

d. State the set of values that represent the domain.

e. State the set of values that represent the range.

Input (x)	Output (y)
0	?
1	?
2	?
3	?
4	?

Exercise 10.4.2

A restaurant seats diners around square tables, where a person can sit at the edge of a table. When two tables are pushed together, six people can sit at the two tables, as shown below.

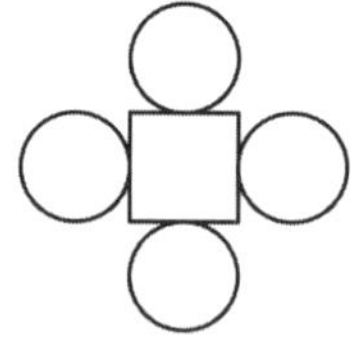
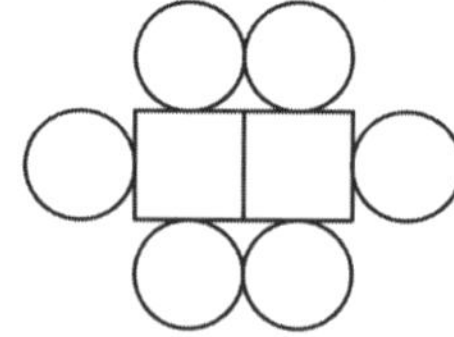
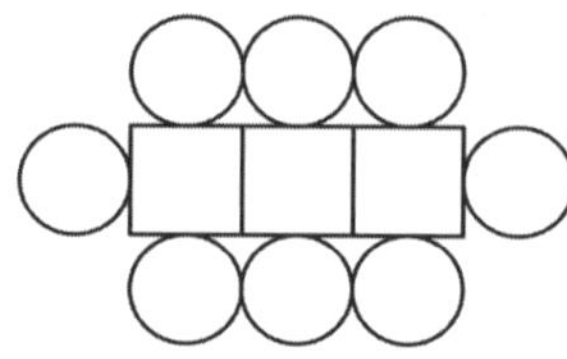

a. Complete the table below to show how many people, y, can sit around tables, where x is the number of tables.

Tables (x)	1	2	3	4	5	6
People (y)	4	6	?	?	?	?

b. Write the x- and y-values as ordered pairs.

c. Plot the points on the Cartesian plane.

d. Determine the rule connecting x and y.

10.5 Transformations

Transformation is a mathematical term used to describe certain changes. Transformations can be numerical, graphical or algebraic. In this section we are going to use our knowledge of coordinates on the Cartesian plane to transform points and shapes.

Coordinates on the Cartesian plane are usually labelled with capital letters, A, for example. When a transformation is applied to a point, causing it to change location on the plane, the resulting point is known as an **image**. An image of a point labelled A is usually labelled A'.

Translation

When we move a point or shape in a positive or negative direction, the movement is called a **translation**. A horizontal translation changes the x-value of a coordinate and a vertical translation changes the y-value of a coordinate.

The diagram shows the triangle ABC translated 5 units to the left and also 4 units down.

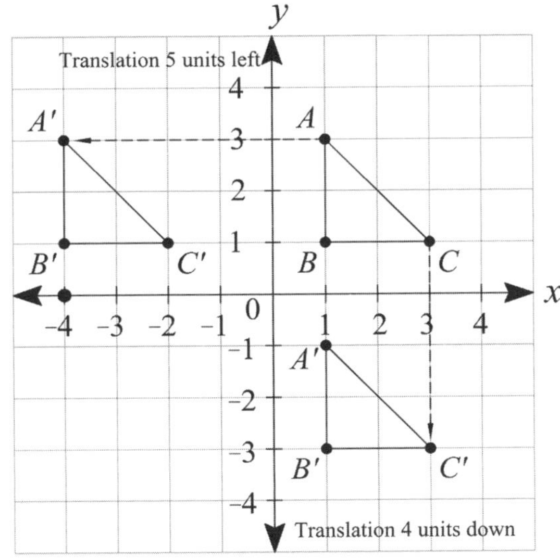

Translation 5 units left

$A(1, 3) \rightarrow A'(-4, 3)$

$B(1, 1) \rightarrow B'(-4, 1)$

$C(3, 1) \rightarrow C'(-2, 1)$

Translation 4 units down

$A(1, 3) \rightarrow A'(1, -1)$

$B(1, 1) \rightarrow B'(1, -3)$

$C(3, 1) \rightarrow C'(3, -3)$

Reflection

When we flip a shape or point across either axis, the movement is called a **reflection**. A reflection in the y-axis changes the sign of the x-value in coordinates and a reflection in the x-axis changes the sign of the y-value in coordinates.

The diagram below shows the triangle ABC reflected in the y-axis and in the x-axis.

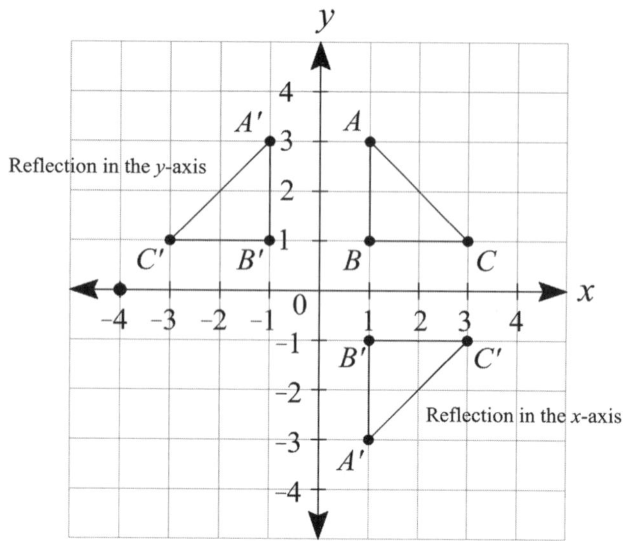

Reflection in the y-axis

$A(1, 3) \rightarrow A'(-1, 3)$

$B(1, 1) \rightarrow B'(-1, 1)$

$C(3, 1) \rightarrow C'(-3, 1)$

Reflection in the x-axis

$A(1, 3) \rightarrow A'(1, -3)$

$B(1, 1) \rightarrow B'(1, -1)$

$C(3, 1) \rightarrow C'(3, -1)$

Example

Consider the diagram below.

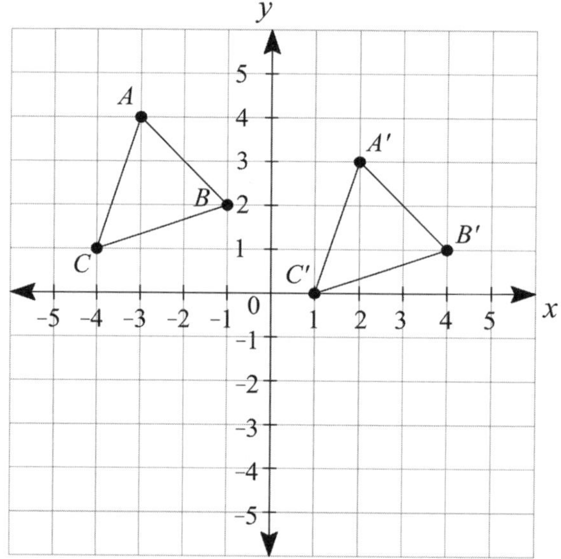

a. Describe a possible set of transformations that will create the image of triangle ABC.

b. Determine the coordinates of A', B' and C'.

c. If the triangle ABC is reflected in the x-axis, determine the coordinates of A', B' and C'.

✓ *Solution*

Working	Explanation
a. Horizontal translation 5 units right, vertical translation 1 unit down.	Select one of the vertices of ABC and count the distance vertically and horizontally to its image.
b. $A(-3, 4) \rightarrow A'(2, 3)$ $B(-1, 2) \rightarrow B'(4, 1)$ $C(-4, 1) \rightarrow C'(1, 0)$	Coordinates are always written (x, y). For each coordinate in ABC, 5 is added to the x-value and 1 is subtracted from the y-value to get the coordinates of the image.
c. $A(-3, 4) \rightarrow A'(-3, -4)$ $B(-1, 2) \rightarrow B'(-1, -2)$ $C(-4, 1) \rightarrow C'(-4, -1)$	A reflection in the x-axis changes the sign of the y-value in the coordinates.

✎ Exercise 10.5.1

Consider the diagram below.

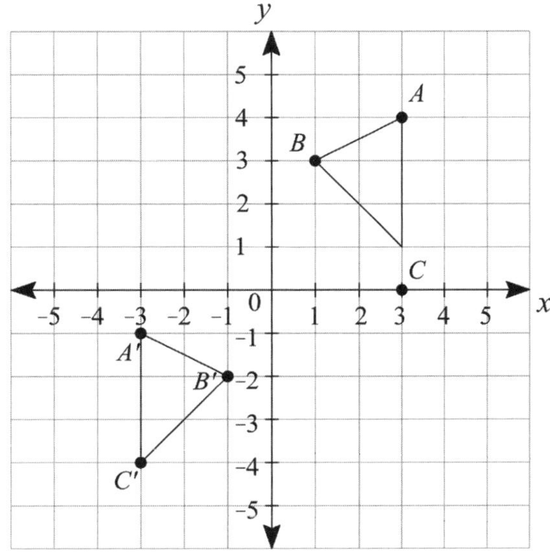

a. Describe a possible set of transformations that will create the image of triangle ABC.

b. Determine the coordinates of A', B' and C'.

c. If the triangle ABC is translated horizontally 2 units in a negative direction, determine the coordinates of A', B' and C'.

Exercise 10.5.2

Consider the diagram below.

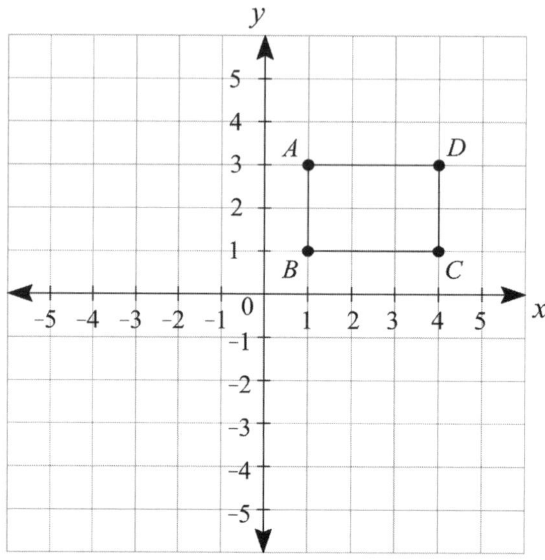

a. Write down the coordinates of A, B, C and D.

b. Determine the coordinates of B' when $ABCD$ is translated 3 units down.

c. Determine the coordinates of A', B', C' and D' if $ABCD$ is reflected in the x-axis and its image is then reflected in the y-axis.

Answers

Exercise 10.1

a. 32, 64, 128

b. 21, 26, 31

c. 12, 9, 6

d. 20, 10, 5

e. 81, 243, 729

f. 30, 36, 42

Exercise 10.2.1

a.

Pattern number (n)	1	2	3	4	5
Number of squares (S)	3	6	10	15	21

b. 28 and 36

Exercise 10.2.2

a.

Pattern number (n)	1	2	3	4	5
Number of squares (S)	6	11	16	21	26

b. $S = 5n + 1$

c. $S = 46$

Exercise 10.3.1

a. output = input × 4 − 2

b. domain: $\{1, 2, 3, 4, 5, 6\}$
range: $\{2, 6, 10, 14, 18, 22\}$

c. output = 38

Exercise 10.3.2

a. output = input × 2 − 3

b. domain: $\{1, 2, 3, 4, 5, 6\}$
range: $\{-1, 1, 3, 5, 7, 9\}$

c. output = 37

Exercise 10.4.1

a.

Input (x)	Output (y)
0	−2
1	−1
2	0
3	1
4	2

b. (0, −2), (1, −1), (2, 0), (3, 1), (4, 2)

c.

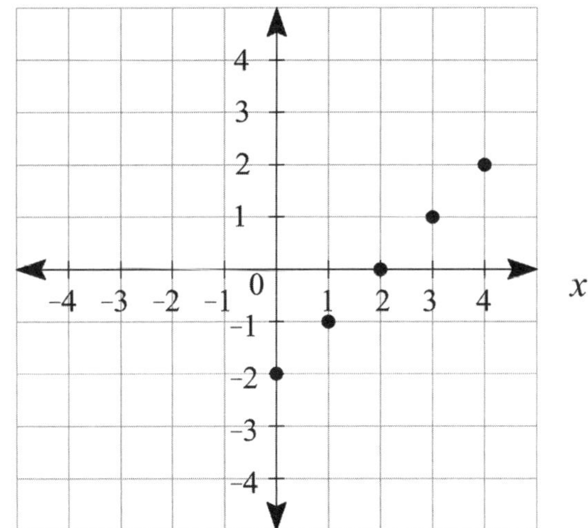

d. domain: $\{0, 1, 2, 3, 4\}$

e. range: $\{-2, -1, 0, 1, 2\}$

Exercise 10.4.2

a.

Tables (x)	1	2	3	4	5	6
People (y)	4	6	8	10	12	14

b. $(1, 4), (2, 6), (3, 8), (4, 10), (5, 12), (6, 14)$

c.

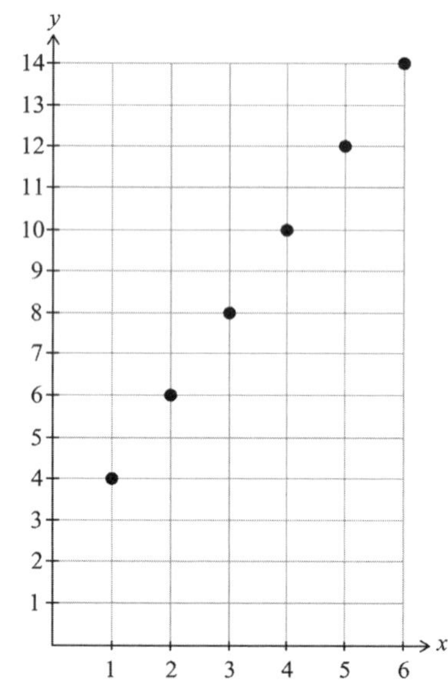

d. $y = 2x + 2$

Exercise 10.5.1

a. Reflection in the y-axis; translation 5 units down.

b. $A'(-3, -1), B'(-1, -2), C'(-3, -4)$

c. $A'(1, 4), B'(-1, 3), C'(1, 1)$

Exercise 10.5.2

a. $A(1, 3), B(1, 1), C(4, 1), D(4, 3)$

b. $B'(1, -2)$

c. $A'(-1, -3), B'(-1, -1), C'(-4, -1), D(-4, -3)$

Chapter 11 – Measurement

Measurement is the study of mathematical concepts related to size. We can measure length, time, weight, height, temperature and many other things.

11.1 Units of length

When measuring **length** we commonly use millimetres (mm), centimetres (cm), metres (m) and kilometres (km) as units.

The following chart may help you convert between the different units of length.

$$10 \text{ millimetres} = 1 \text{ centimetre}$$

$$100 \text{ centimetres} = 1 \text{ metre}$$

$$1000 \text{ metres} = 1 \text{ kilometre}$$

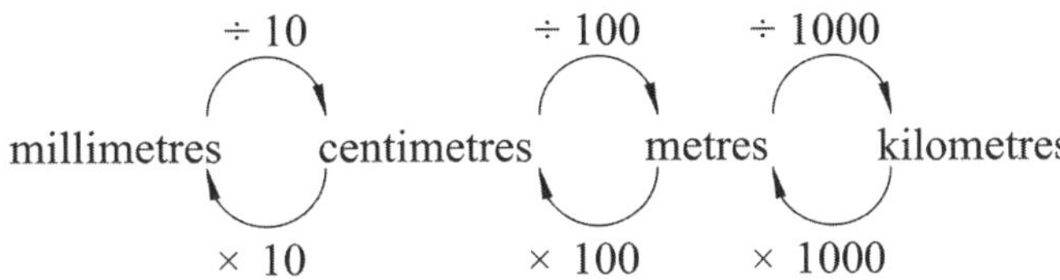

Example

a. Write 6 m in centimetres.

b. Write 780 m in kilometres.

c. Add 45.2 cm and 87 mm, giving your answer in millimetres.

✓ *Solution*

Working	Explanation
a. $6 \times 100 = 600$ 600 cm	To convert from metres to centimetres we multiply by 100 (as shown in the conversion chart above). Write the answer with the requested unit of measurement.
b. $780 \div 1000 = 0.78$ 0.78 km	To convert from metres to kilometres we divide by 1000. Write the answer with the requested unit of measurement.
c. $45.2 \times 10 = 452$ $452 + 87 = 539$ 539 mm	First convert 45.2 cm to millimetres. Add the two values. Write the answer with the requested unit of measurement.

Exercise 11.1.1

Complete the following conversions.

a. 560 mm = ______ m **b.** 3.6 km = ______ m

c. 90 cm = ______ m **d.** 8.7 cm = ______ mm

Exercise 11.1.2

a. A gum tree is measured to be 345 cm high. What is the height of the tree in metres?

b. One walking lap around a lake is 5.8 km. How many metres is two laps of the lake?

11.2 Perimeter

Perimeter is the distance around the outside of a flat shape. To calculate the perimeter we add up all the individual side lengths.

Example

Find the perimeter of each of the following shapes.

a.

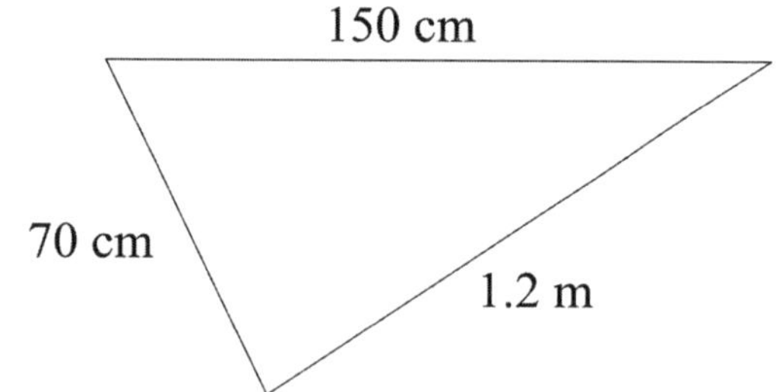

b.

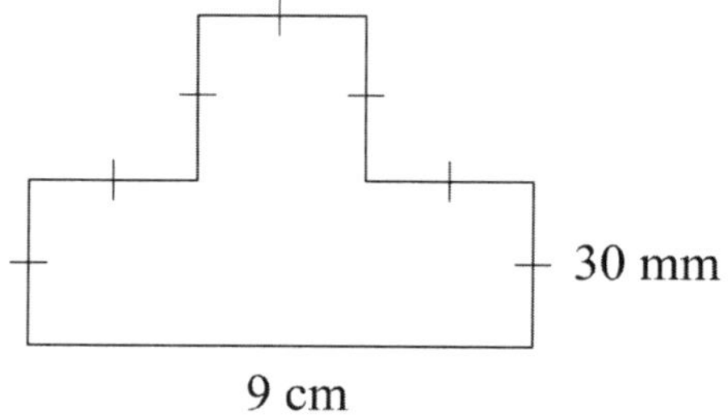

✓ *Solution*

Working	Explanation
a. 1.2 m = 120 cm $P = 70 + 150 + 120$ $= 340$ cm	Convert each side length to the same unit of measurement. The perimeter is the sum of all three sides. State the unit of measurement in the final step of the calculation.
b. 30 mm = 3 cm	Before calculating the perimeter of any shape, we must convert the length of each side to the same unit of measurement.
$P = 9 + (3 \times 7)$ $= 9 + 21$ $= 30$ cm	Recall the notation on sides that indicates that they are of equal length. When this notation appears, multiplication can be used instead of repeated addition. In this example 7 sides are of equal length. State the unit of measurement in the final step of the calculation.

Exercise 11.2

a. Calculate the perimeter of a rectangular laptop with a length of 25 cm and a width of 33 cm.

b. A netball court measures 30.5 m by 15.25 m. Calculate the perimeter of the court.

c. Calculate the perimeter of the following shape.

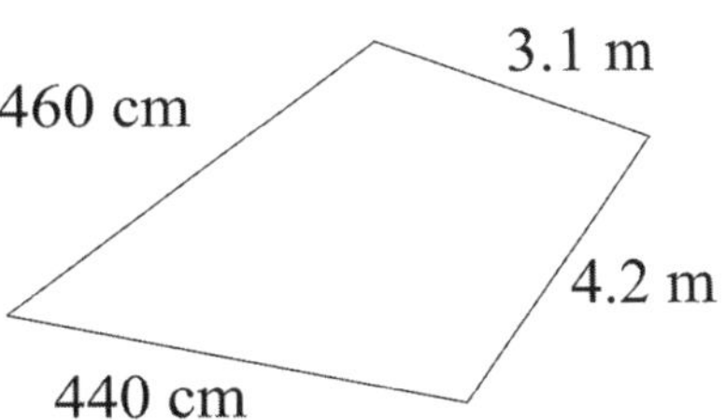

11.3 Area

In the previous section we calculated the perimeter as the total length of the sides of a flat shape. Area can be considered as the total space inside the shape.

When measuring area we commonly use such square units as mm^2, cm^2, m^2 and km^2.

The following table shows how to calculate the area of some common shapes.

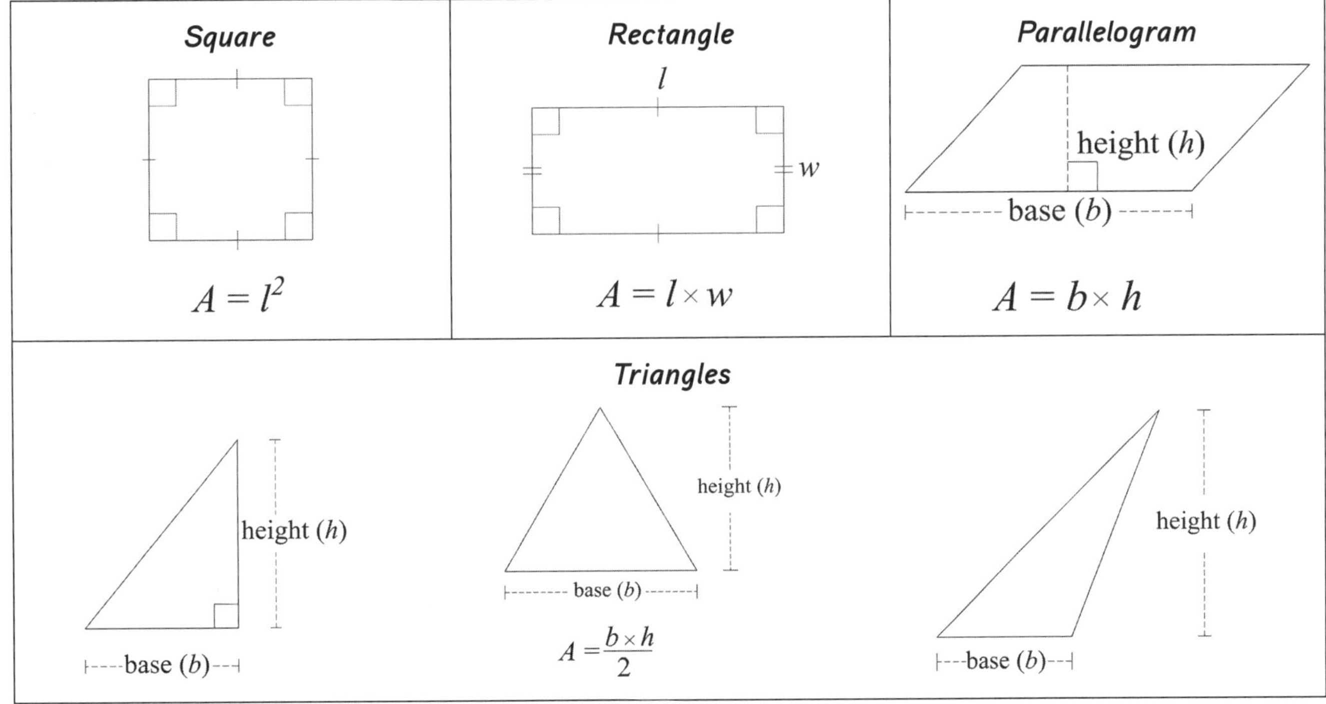

Example

Calculate the area of the following shapes.

a.

23 cm

150 mm

b.

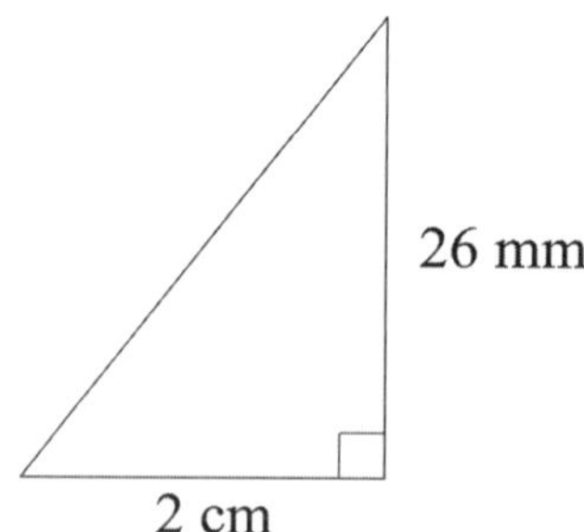

✓ Solution

Working	Explanation
a. 150 mm $=$ 15 cm	Before calculating the area of any shape, we must convert each side length to the same unit.
$A = 23 \times 15$ $= 345\ \text{cm}^2$	The formula for the area of a rectangle is $A = l \times w$. Remember to include the appropriate unit of measurement: cm^2.
b. 2 cm $=$ 20 mm	Before calculating the area of any shape, we must convert each side length to the same unit.
$A = \frac{1}{2} \times 20 \times 26$ $= 10 \times 26$ $= 260\ \text{mm}^2$	The formula for the area of a triangle is $A = \frac{1}{2} \times b \times h$. Remember to include the appropriate unit of measurement: mm^2.

Exercise 11.3

a. Calculate the area of a rectangular room that is 4.1 m wide and 3.6 m long.

b. Calculate the area of a triangular ‘give way’ road sign that has a height of 78 cm and a base of 90 cm.

c. What is the perimeter of a rectangle that has an area of 21 cm^2 and a width of 7 cm?

11.4 Area of composite shapes

A **composite** shape is one made up of two or more other shapes.

We find the area of a composite shape by breaking the shape into simpler shapes and then adding or subtracting the areas.

Example

a.

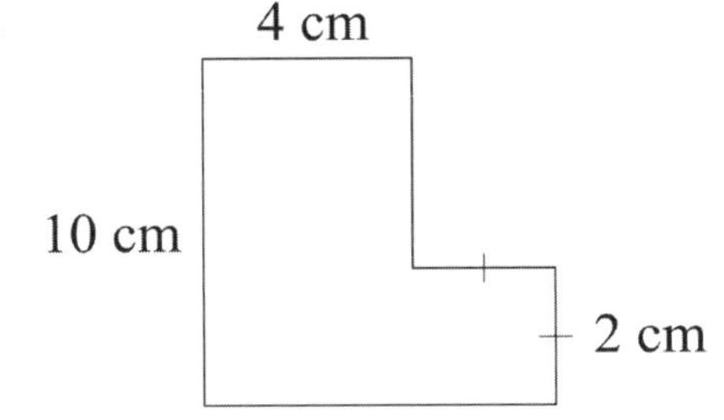

b.

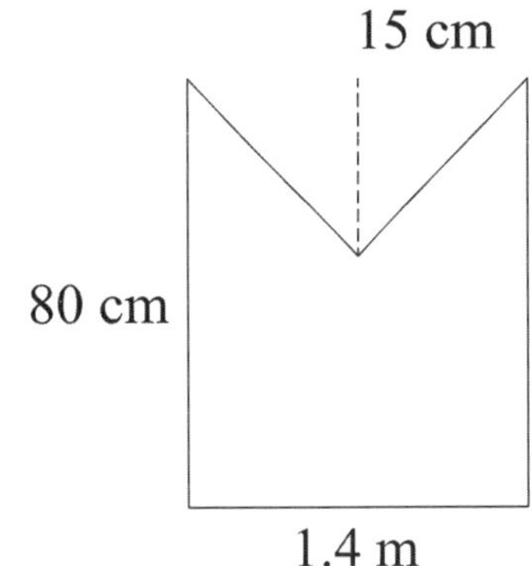

✓ Solution

Working	Explanation
a. 4 cm, 10 cm, A_1, A_2, 2 cm	Break the composite shape into a rectangle (A_1) and a square (A_2). Since all lengths are in the same unit, no conversion is necessary before calculating the area.
$A_1 = 10 \times 4 = 40$ $A_2 = 2 \times 2 = 4$ $A_{\text{total}} = 44\ \text{cm}^2$	Calculate the area of each individual shape. Add the two areas to get the total area of the composite shape. Include the appropriate unit of measurement.

b. 80 cm; A_1; 1.4 m; 1.4 m; A_2; 15 cm	Break the composite shape into a rectangle (A_1) and a triangle (A_2).
$A_1 = 80 \times 140$ $= 11\,200$ $A_2 = \frac{1}{2} \times 140 \times 15$ $= 1050$	Convert all lengths into the same unit of measurement and then calculate the areas individually.
$A_{\text{total}} = 11\,200 - 1050$ $= 10\,150 \text{ cm}^2$	Subtract the area of the triangle from the area of the rectangle (because we are removing that section from the rectangle to make the composite shape). Include the appropriate unit of measurement.

Exercise 11.4

Calculate the area of the following composite shapes.

a.

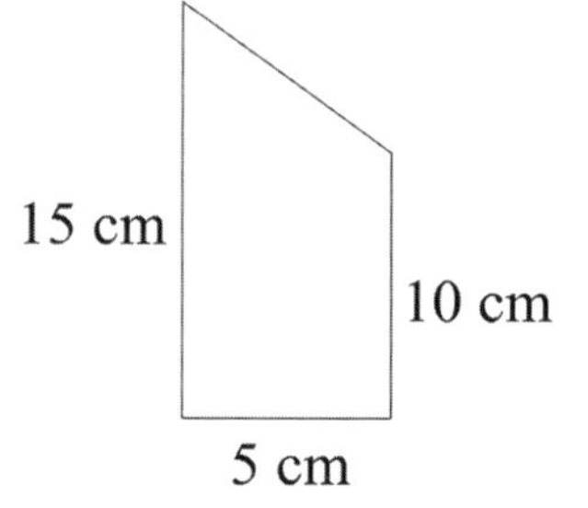

b.

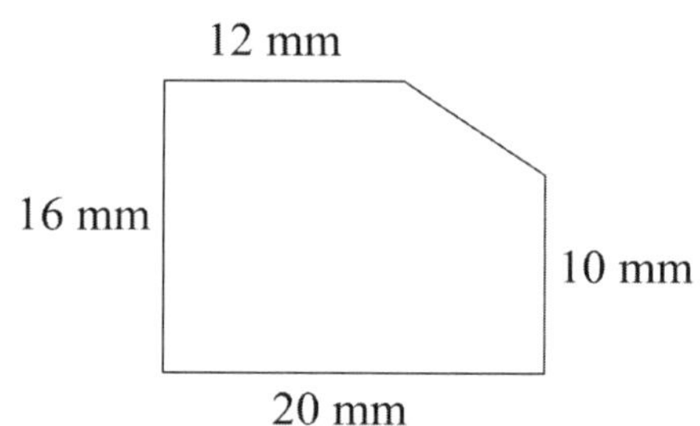

c.

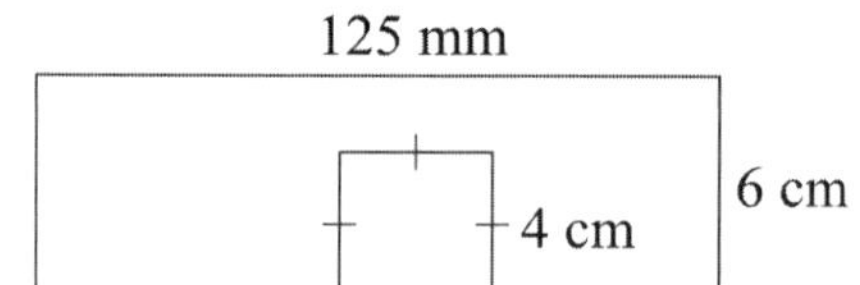

11.5 Volume

Volume is the measurement of the space inside a three-dimensional object.

A common three-dimensional object is a **prism** (such as a cube). We calculate the volume (V) of a prism using the formula

$$V = L \times W \times H$$

where L is the length, W is the width and H is the height of the prism.

When measuring volume, we commonly use such cubic units as mm^3, cm^3, m^3 and km^3.

Example

Calculate the volume of the following prism.

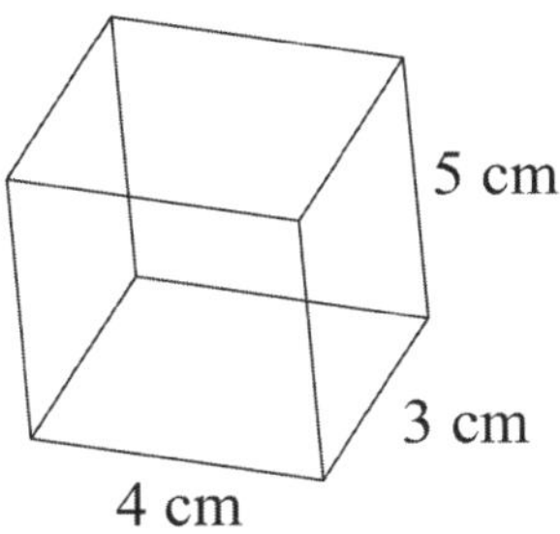

✓ *Solution*

Working	Explanation
$V = 4 \times 3 \times 5$ $= 60$ cm^3	Given that all the dimensions are in the same unit of measurement, we can substitute the values directly into the formula without conversion. Calculate the solution using the formula $V = L \times W \times H$ and add the appropriate unit of measurement.

Exercise 11.5

a. Calculate the volume of a shipping container with the dimensions 3 metres wide, 6 metres long and 2.4 metres high.

b. A rectangular lap pool is being installed in a backyard. The dimensions of the hole are 12 metres long, 2.5 metres wide, and 2 metres deep. Calculate the volume of dirt that has been removed.

Answers

Exercise 11.1.1

a. 0.56 m b. 3600 m c. 0.9 m d. 87 mm

Exercise 11.1.2

a. 3.45 m b. 11 600 m

Exercise 11.2

a. 116 cm b. 91.5 m c. 1630 cm or 16.30 m

Exercise 11.3

a. 14.76 m^2 b. 3510 cm^2 c. 20 cm

Exercise 11.4

a. 62.5 cm^2 b. 296 mm^2 c. 59 cm^2 or 5900 mm^2

Exercise 11.5

a. 43.2 m^3 b. 60 m^3

Chapter 12 – Geometry

Geometry is the mathematical study of shapes and lines. It is interested in the properties of angles, lines and planes, such as where they intersect, and how they change when rotated, reflected and translated.

12.1 Geometric notation

The geometric symbol ∠ means 'angle'. If we use the notation $\angle ABC$, then:

- the capital letters represent the **vertices** of a shape and
- the letter in the middle is the **vertex** at the angle whose size we are trying to find.

Lower case letters are used to represent the sides that are opposite the vertex of the same letter. For example, the side opposite vertex B will be labelled b.

Example

Consider the following triangle.

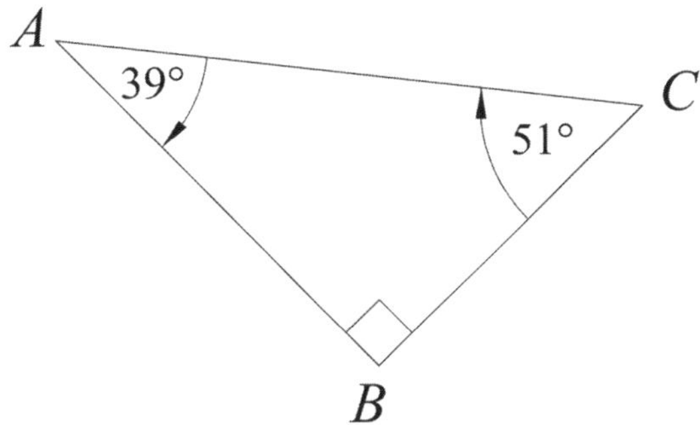

a. Determine $\angle CAB$. **b.** Determine $\angle ACB$. **c.** Determine $\angle ABC$.

✓ *Solution*

Working	Explanation
a. 39°	From the order of the letters, we can tell that $\angle CAB$ means the angle at vertex A. Always add the degree symbol after an angle measurement.
b. 51°	From the order of the letters, we can tell that $\angle ACB$ means the angle at vertex C.
c. 90°	$\angle ABC$ means that the angle of interest is the angle at vertex B. The square in the corner of the angle is the mathematical symbol for 90°.

Exercise 12.1.1

Determine $\angle ABC$.

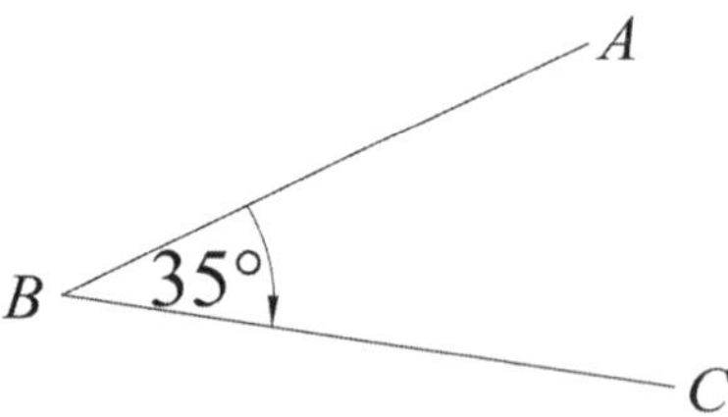

Exercise 12.1.2

Consider the following triangle.

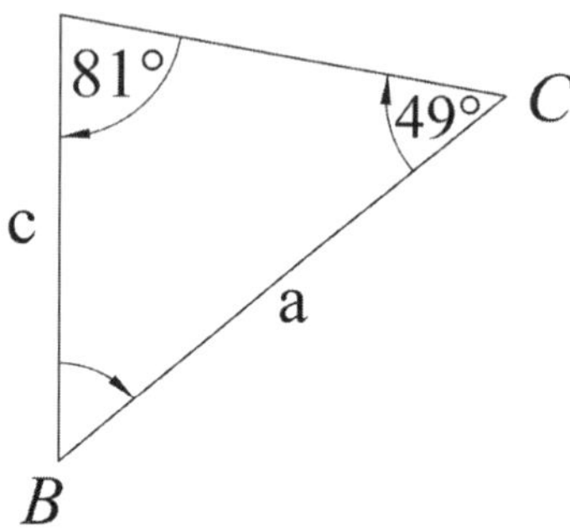

a. Complete the labelling of the vertices and the sides.

b. Determine $\angle CAB$.

c. Determine $\angle ACB$.

d. Determine $\angle ABC$

12.2 Angles at a point

When lines intersect (or meet) at a point, there are certain geometric properties that can be determined without the use of a protractor. The following table explains some of these properties.

When multiple lines meet at a point and the sum of the angles between them is 90°, the angles are called **complementary** angles.	When multiple lines meet at a point and the sum of the angles between them is 180°, the angles are called **supplementary** angles.	When two lines cross, the angles opposite the point of intersection (known as **opposite angles**) have the same magnitude (size).
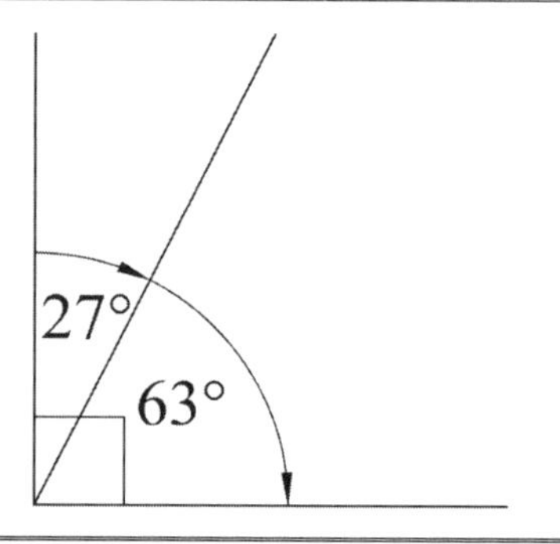	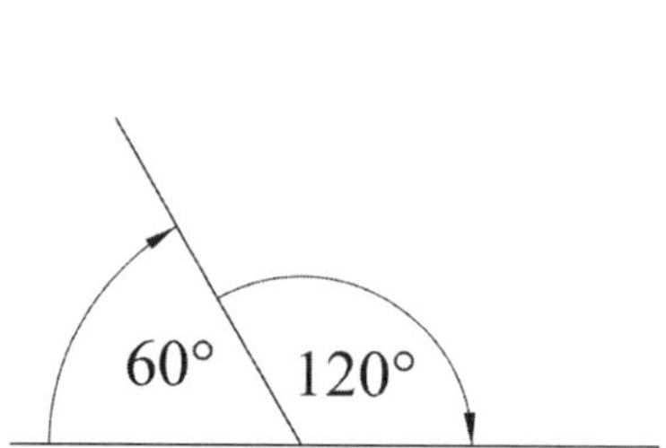	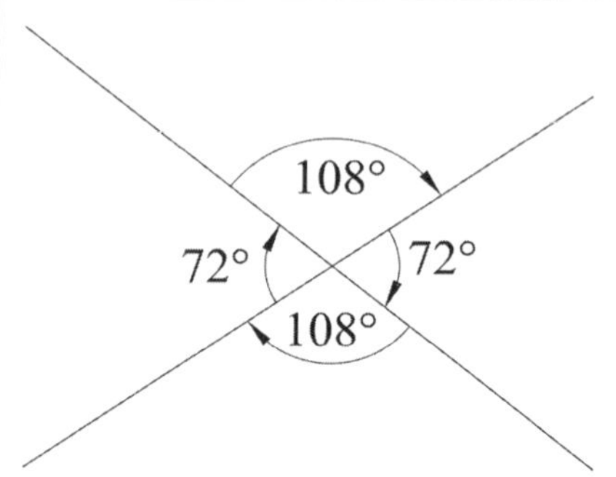

Example

Determine the size of the unknown angles in the following diagrams without using a protractor.

a.

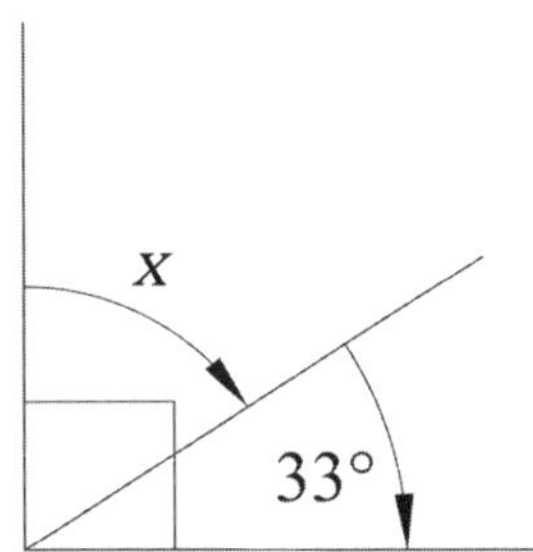

b.

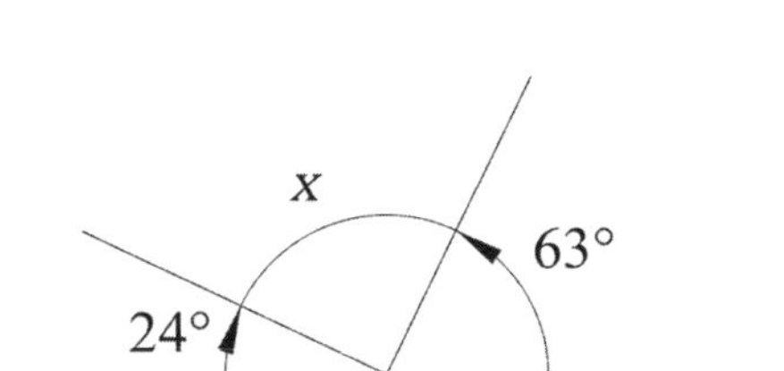

c.

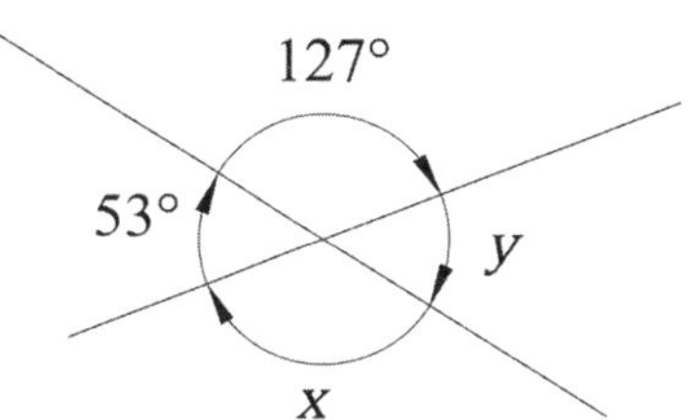

✓ Solution

Working	Explanation
a. $x + 33 = 90$ $x = 57°$	The square indicates that the vertical and horizontal lines meet at 90°. Therefore the angles between the three lines are complementary angles.
b. $24 + x + 63 = 180$ $x = 93°$	The horizontal line is 180°, therefore the angles between the lines meeting at a point on the horizontal line are supplementary angles.
c. $x = 127°$ $y = 53°$	Intersecting lines create opposite angles and opposite angles are equal.

Exercise 12.2.1

Determine the value of x in the following diagrams.

a.

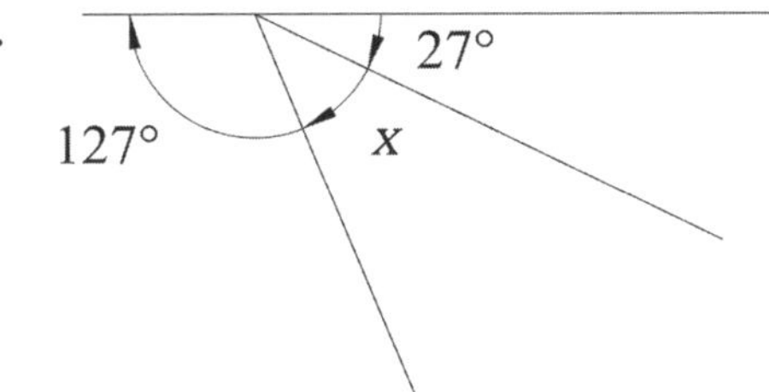

b.

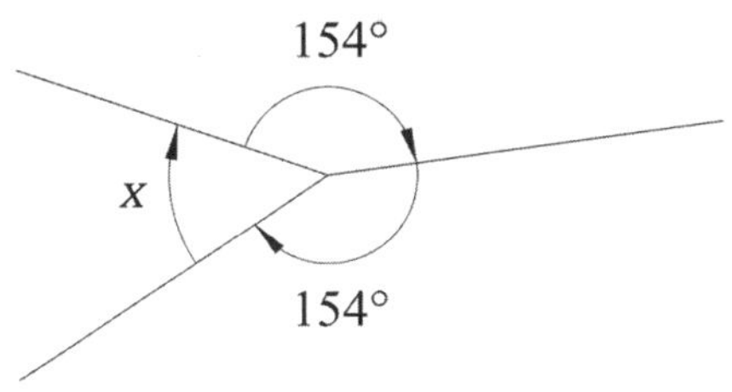

Exercise 12.2.2

Determine the value of $\angle AOB$ in the following diagram.

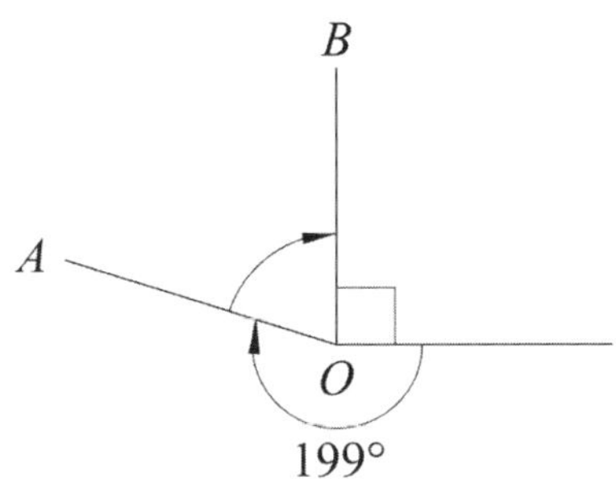

12.3 Parallel lines

To indicate that lines are parallel, they are marked with arrows in diagrams. An example is in the diagram below, where lines AB and CD are parallel. The mathematical symbol for parallel is ||, as in $AB \parallel CD$.

A line that crosses two or more parallel lines is called a **transversal** line.

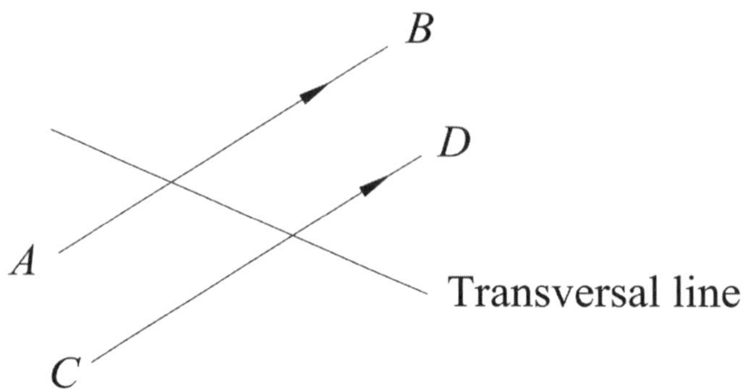

The angles created by a transversal line and a set of parallel lines have the following geometric properties.

Alternate angles are angles that are: • on opposite sides of the transversal line and • in the opposite position. Alternate angles are equal.	**Corresponding** angles are angles that are: • on the same side of the transversal line and • in the same position. Corresponding angles are equal.	**Co-interior** angles are angles that are: • on the same side of the transversal line and • inside the parallel lines. The sum of co-interior angles is $180°$.
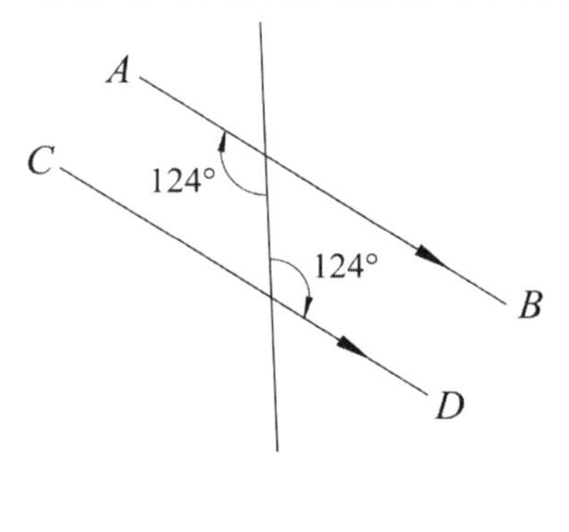	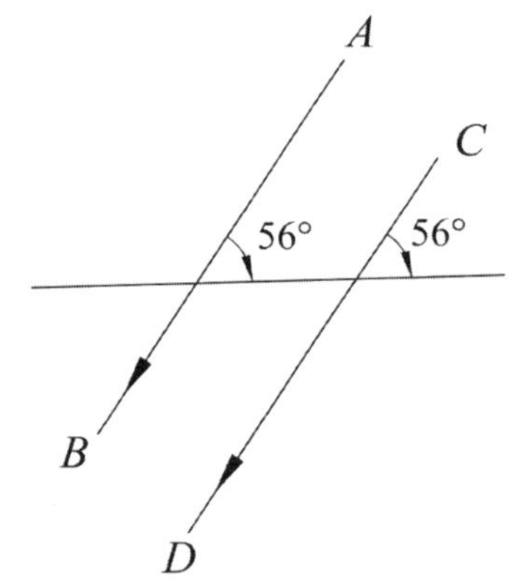	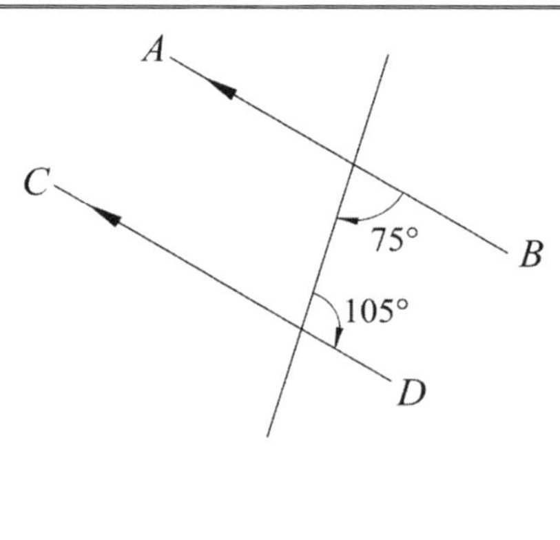

Example

Using the geometric properties of parallel lines discussed on the previous page, calculate the size of the unknown angles in the diagram below.

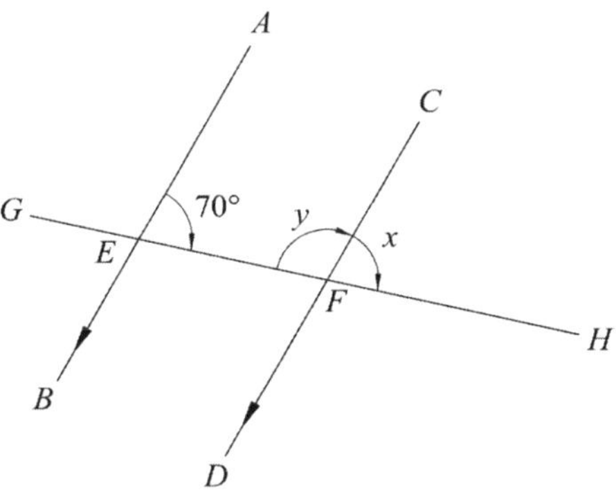

✓ ***Solution***

Working	Explanation
$x = 70°$	$\angle AEH$ and $\angle CFH$ are corresponding angles and therefore equal.
$70 + y = 180$ $y = 110°$	$\angle AEH$ and $\angle CFG$ are co-interior angles and thus sum to $180°$.

Exercise 12.3

Consider the following diagram.

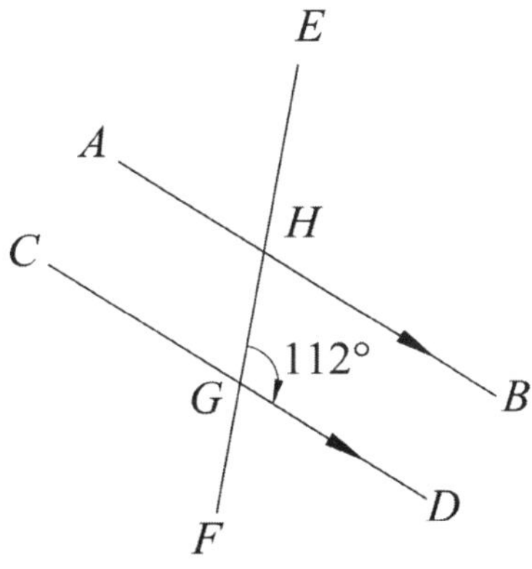

Determine the size of the following angles.

a. $\angle EHB$ **b.** $\angle FHB$ **c.** $\angle CGE$ **d.** $\angle CGF$ **e.** $\angle AHE$

12.4 Polygons

A **polygon** is any two-dimensional shape made up of straight lines.

We can classify polygons as **regular** or **irregular** based on the geometric properties of the angles made by the connecting sides.

Regular polygons are shapes with multiple sides of the same length and with equal **interior angles**. A pentagon and a rectangle (shown below) are regular polygons. 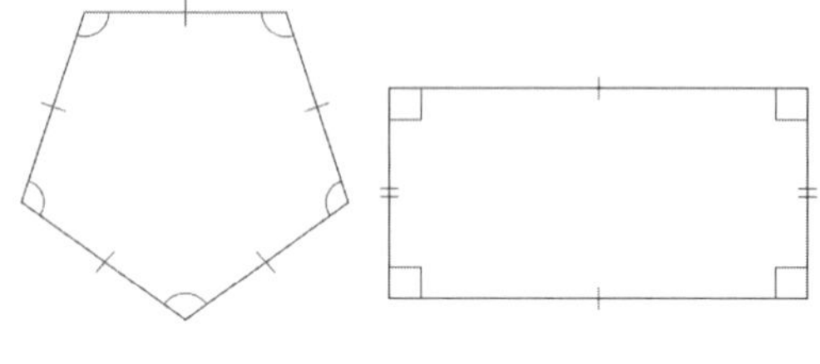	**Irregular polygons** are shapes with straight sides that do not have equal geometric properties. Irregular polygons are **convex** if the vertices all face outwards or **concave** if at least one vertex faces inwards. 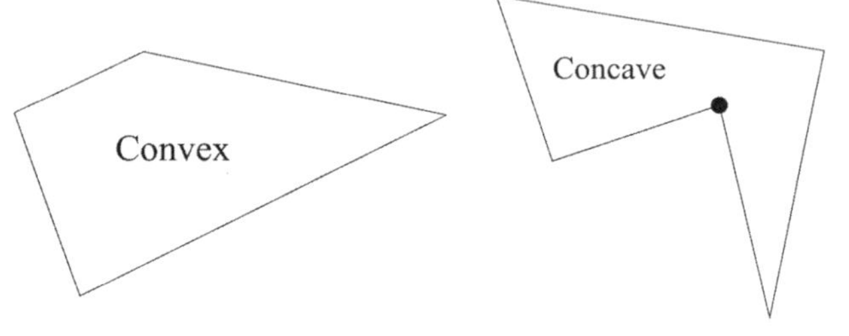

Example

Consider the regular polygon shown below.

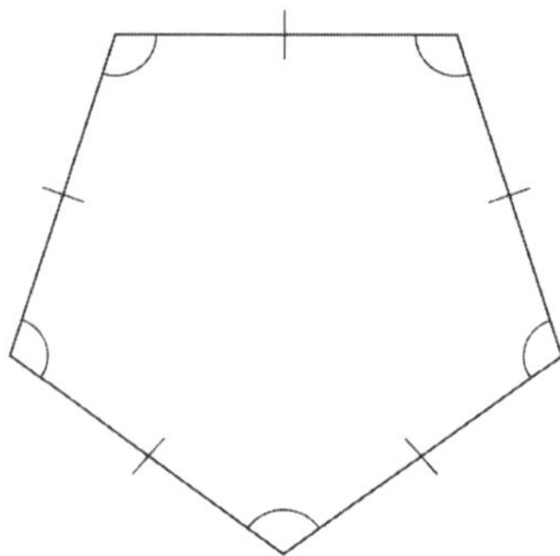

a. Calculate the sum of the interior angles.

b. Calculate the size of an interior angle.

Solution

Working	Explanation
a. $180(5-2) = 180 \times 3$ $= 540°$	The formula for the sum of the interior angles of a regular polygon is $$180 \times (n-2)$$ where n is the number of sides. A regular polygon has 5 sides, so $n = 5$.
b. $540 \div 5 = 108°$	The formula for the size of an interior angle in a regular polygon is $$a = s \div n$$ where a is the interior angle, s is the sum of all the interior angles and n is the number of sides.

Exercise 12.4

Consider each of the regular polygons shown below.

i. Calculate the sum of the interior angles.

ii. Calculate the size of each interior angle.

a.

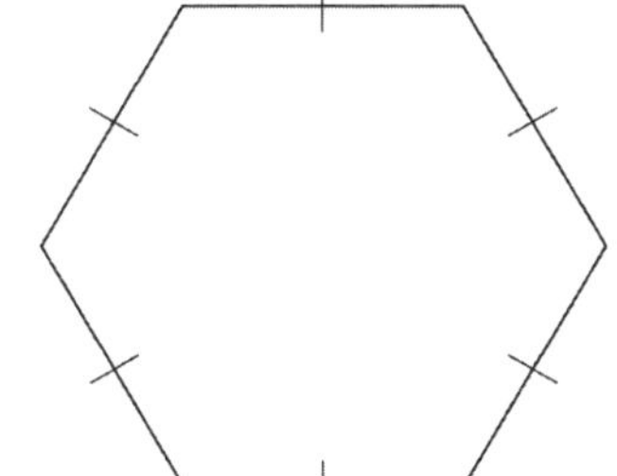

b.

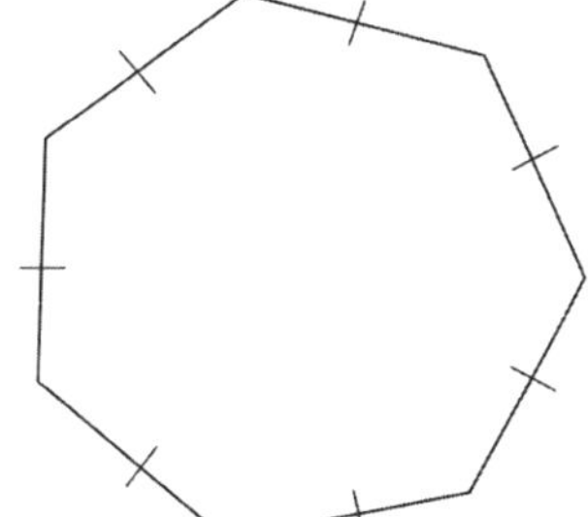

c.

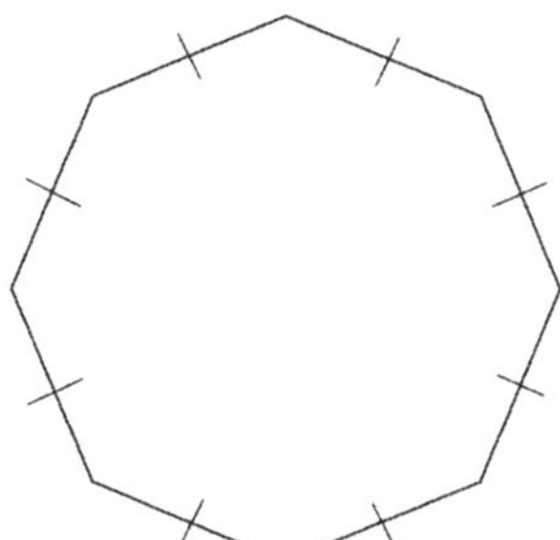

12.5 Triangles

Just as vertices can be referred to by the capital letter notation explained earlier, triangles can be referred to by the same notation. For example, if the vertices of a triangle are labelled A, B and C, the triangle can be referred to as ΔABC.

The table below lists some of the properties of different triangles.

Scalene triangle ΔABC	**Isosceles triangle** ΔDEF	**Equilateral triangle** ΔGHI	**Right-angle triangle** ΔJKL
All sides and angles are different.	Two sides are the same length and the base angles are the same size.	All sides are the same length and all angles are the same size.	Two sides meet at 90°.

The sum of the interior angles of a triangle is 180°. The adjacent exterior angle (d in the diagram below) can be found using an interesting geometric property, illustrated below.

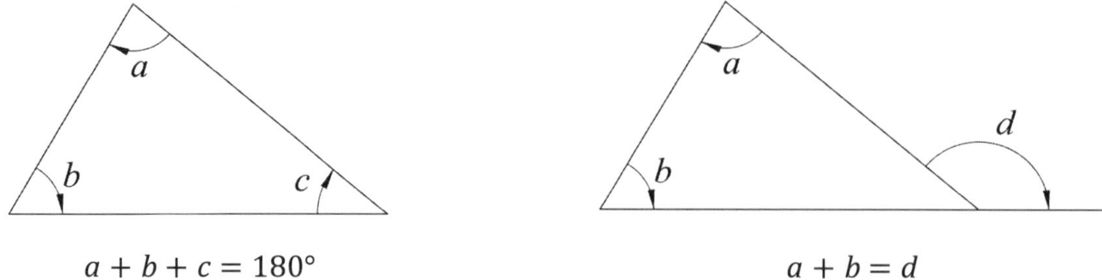

$a + b + c = 180°$ $\qquad$ $a + b = d$

Example

Calculate the size of the unknown angles in the diagram below.

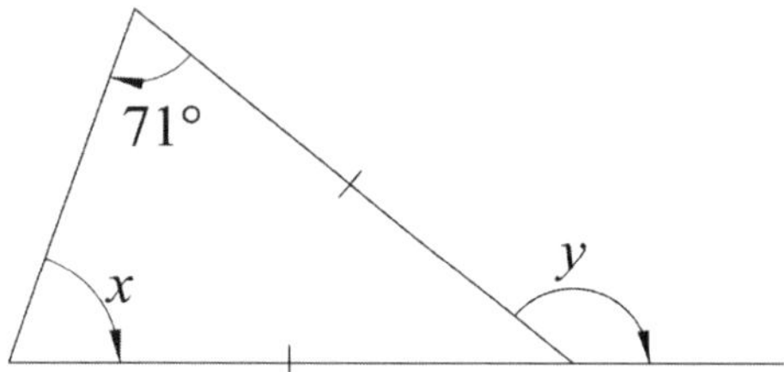

✓ *Solution*

Working	Explanation
$x = 71°$	The shape is an isosceles triangle, so the base angles must be equal in size.
$71 + 71 = y$ $y = 142°$	The exterior angle y can be found from the property of adjacent exterior angles illustrated.

Exercise 12.5

Calculate the unknown angles in the diagram below.

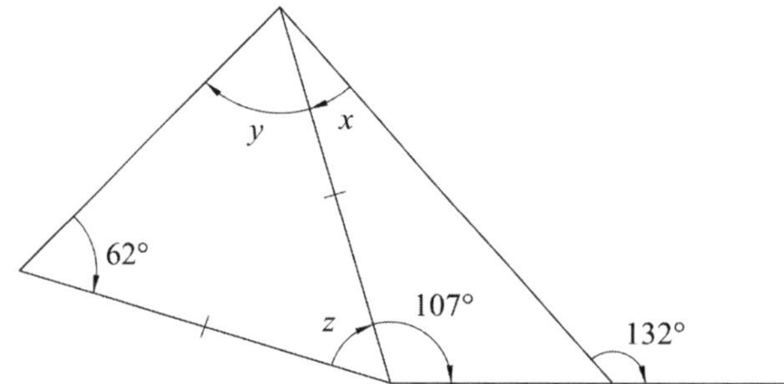

12.6 Quadrilaterals

Any four-sided polygon is called a **quadrilateral**.

The sum of the interior angles in a quadrilateral is 360°, as they can be divided into two triangles.

The table below lists some of the properties of common quadrilaterals.

Square	Rectangle	Parallelogram
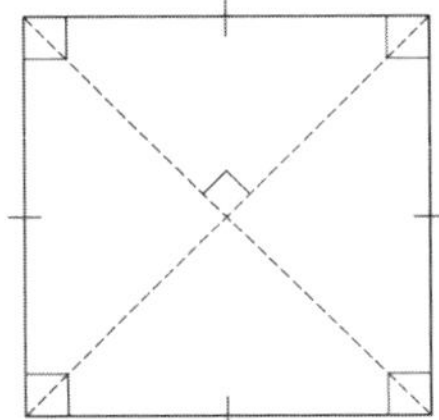	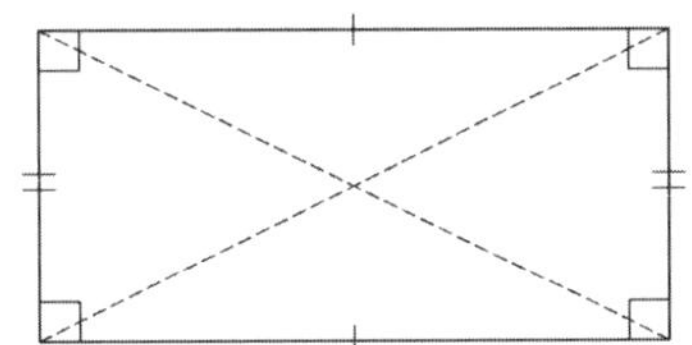	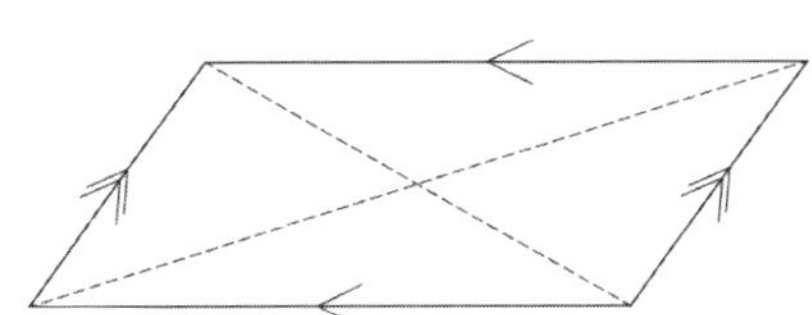
• All sides are equal. • All interior angles are 90°. • The diagonals bisect at 90°.	• Opposite sides are equal but the lengths of each pair are different. • All interior angles are 90°.	• Opposite sides are equal but the lengths of each pair are different. • Two pairs of sides are parallel. • Opposite angles are equal.
Rhombus	**Kite**	**Trapezium**
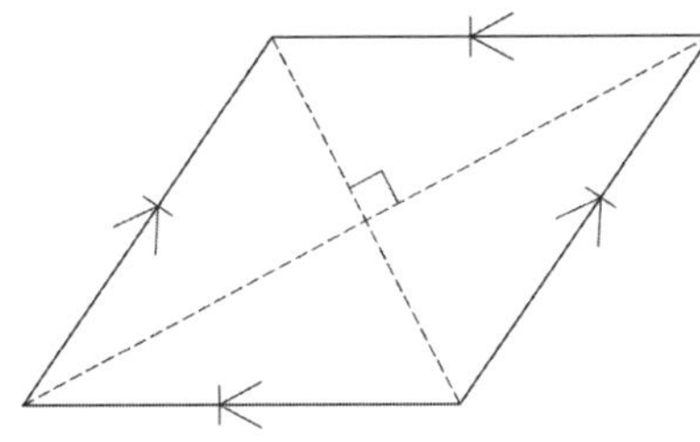	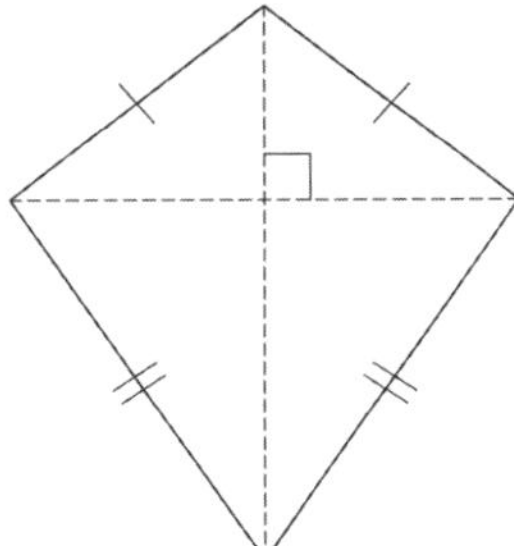	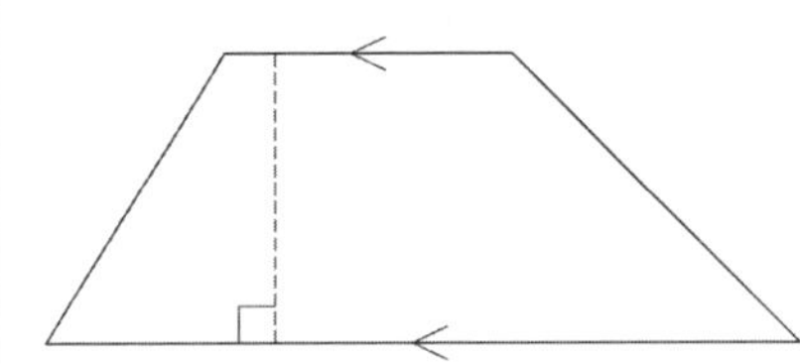
• All sides are equal. • Each pair of sides is parallel. • The diagonals bisect at 90°.	• Two pairs of sides are equal. • The diagonals bisect at 90°.	• One pair of sides is parallel. • Sides can be different lengths.

Example

Determine the unknown angle in the following quadrilateral.

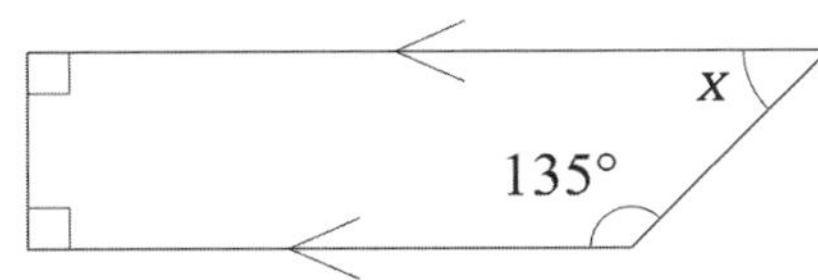

✓ Solution

Working	Explanation
$90 + 90 + 135 + x = 360$ $x = 45°$	The sum of the internal angles of a quadrilateral is 360°.

Exercise 12.6

Determine the unknown angles in the following diagram.

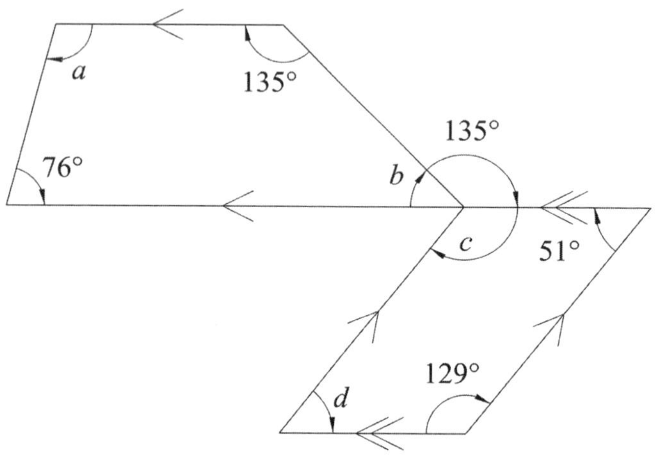

12.7 Solids and nets

A **solid** is a three-dimensional object constructed of two-dimensional shapes. A **net** is the shapes that make up the solid.

It is important to understand which solids can be unfolded to make two-dimensional nets, and which nets can be folded to make three-dimensional solids.

In the table below, the top row shows some common solids and the bottom row shows the corresponding net for each solid.

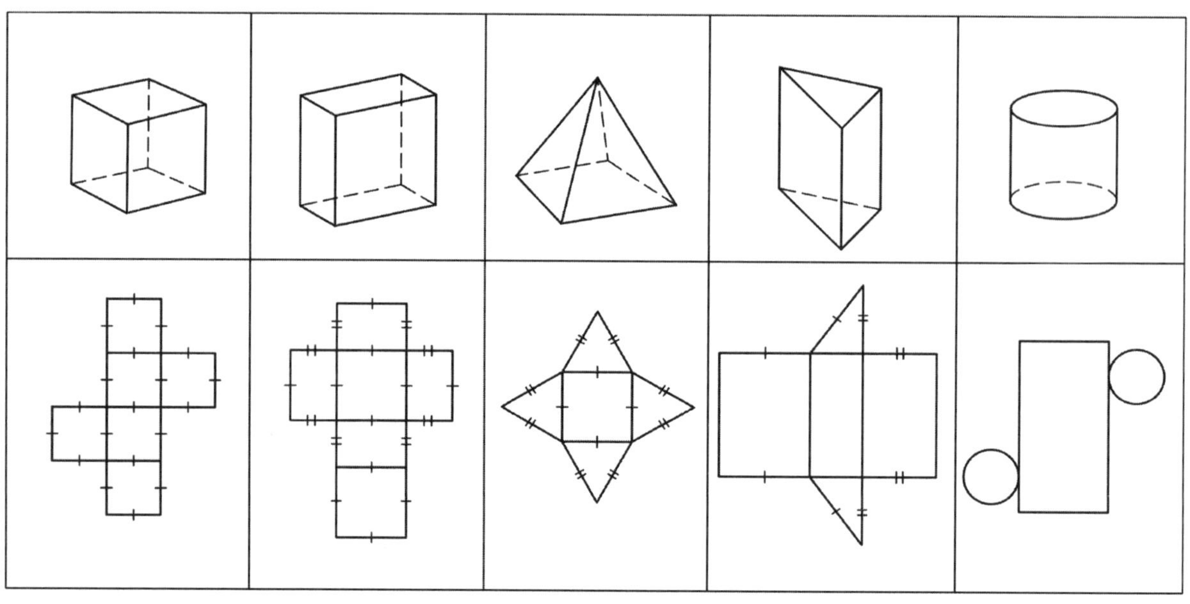

Example

Describe the difference between the net of a cube and the net of a square-based rectangular prism.

✓ *Solution*

Working	Explanation
A cube is composed of six identical squares whereas a square-based rectangular prism is composed of two square ends and four identical rectangles.	If you think about prisms as nets, it is easier to see the similarities and differences between them. **Note**: a cube is a type of prism.

Exercise 12.7

Name the solid that can be created by folding each of the following nets.

a.

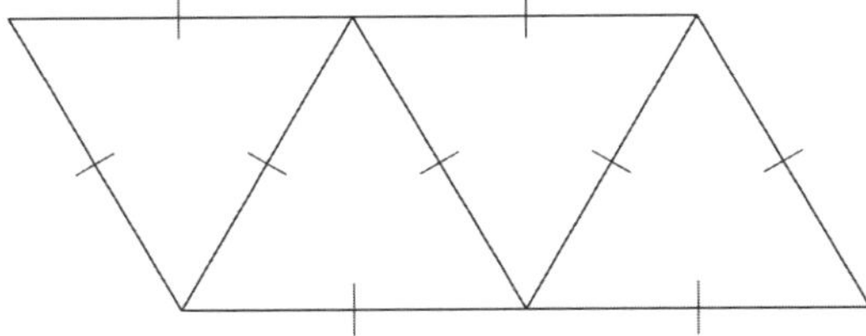

b.

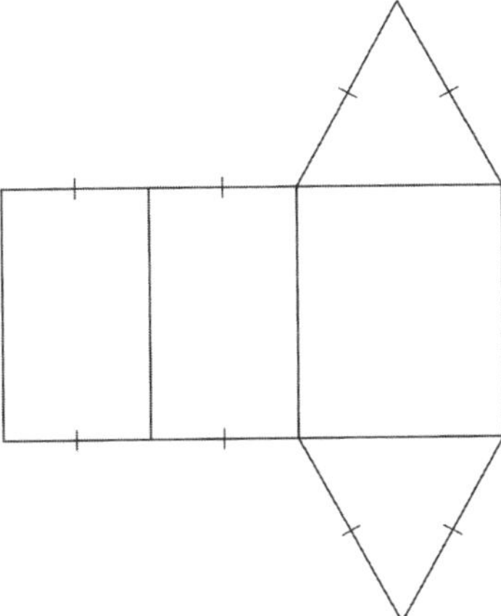

c.

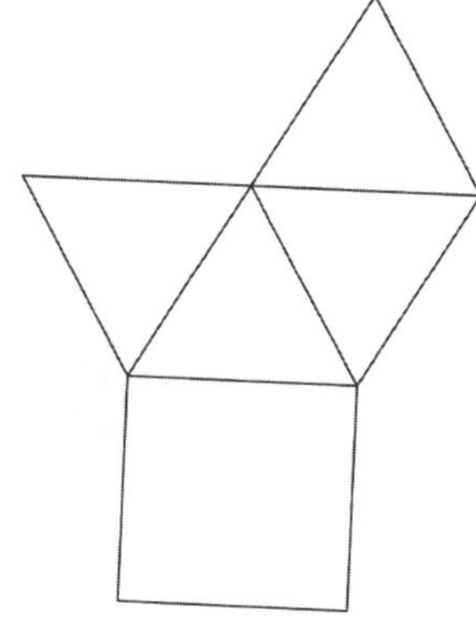

12.8 Circle geometry

A circle is a shape that is perfectly symmetrical about a **centre** point.

The **radius** extends from the centre of a circle to any point on the circle's circumference.

The **diameter** passes through the centre of a circle and extends from any point on its circumference to any other point on its circumference. It is the length of two radii.

The **circumference** is the distance around the circle.

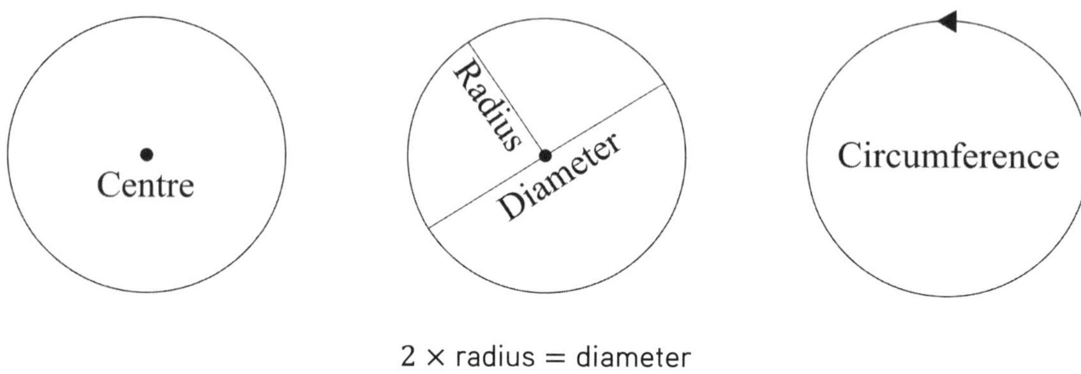

2 × radius = diameter

circumference ÷ diameter = π

Example

Twenty school students in a sport class are standing in a circle. The distance from one side to the other through the centre of the circle is 8 metres.

Calculate the radius and circumference of the circle. Use a calculator and round the answer to one decimal place.

✓ Solution

Working	Explanation
$d \div 2 = r$ $8 \div 2 = 4$ m	The radius (r) of any circle is half the diameter (d).
$C = \pi \times d$ $= \pi \times 8$ $= 25.1$ m	The circumference (C) can be found after rearranging the formula given above.

Example

Ten more students join the circle described in the previous example. They make the radius 6 metres and the circumference approximately 37.7 m.

Determine an approximate value for pi (π).

✓ ***Solution***

Working	Explanation
$37.7 \div 12 \approx 3.141...$ $\approx \pi$	The radius is now 6 m, which makes the diameter 12 m. Dividing the circumference by the diameter will give an approximate value for pi.

Exercise 12.8

The radius of a circle is doubled from 15 cm to 30 cm. By how much does the circumference of the circle increase?

Answers

Exercise 12.1.1

$\angle ABC = 35°$

Exercise 12.1.2

a. 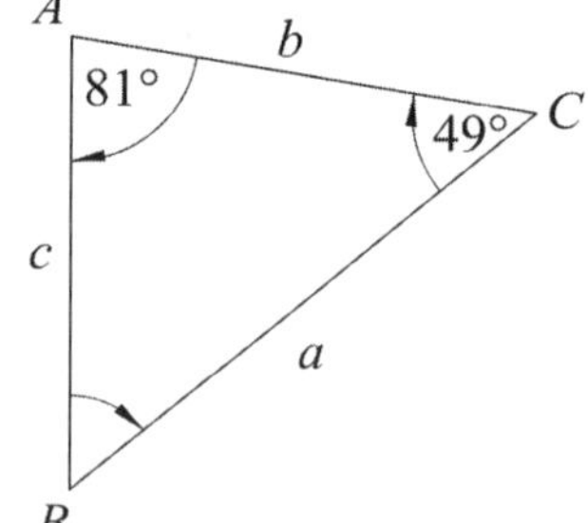

b. $\angle CAB = 81°$

c. $\angle ACB = 49°$

d. $\angle ABC = 50°$

Exercise 12.2.1

a. $x = 26°$

b. $x = 52°$

Exercise 12.2.2

$\angle AOB = 71°$

Exercise 12.3

a. $\angle EHB = 112°$

b. $\angle FHB = 68°$

c. $\angle CGE = 68°$

d. $\angle CGF = 112°$

e. $\angle AHE = 68°$

Exercise 12.4

a. i. $720°$ ii. $120°$

b. i. $900°$ ii. $\approx 129°$ (rounded)

c. i. $1080°$ ii. $135°$

Exercise 12.5

$x = 25°, y = 62°, z = 56°$

Exercise 12.6

$a = 104°, b = 45°, c = 129°, d = 51°$

Exercise 12.7

a. triangular-based pyramid

b. triangular prism

c. square-based pyramid

Exercise 12.8

$30\pi \approx 94.247...$

$60\pi \approx 188.495...$

By doubling the length of the radius, the circumference doubles in length, as pi is a constant.

Chapter 13 – Statistics

Statistics is the mathematics behind many scientific studies. It is the collection, analysis and presentation of data. In this chapter we discuss the types of data that are collected, some techniques for analysing and interpreting what data is telling us, and ways of presenting data in the form of graphs that are informative and can easily be read.

13.1 Numerical data

Numerical data is data that results from measuring or counting. It is always expressed in numbers. Height, weight, test scores, time, speed and distance are all examples of numerical data. The colours of jellybeans in a jar or the types of cars on the road are not numerical data.

Numerical data can be whole numbers, fractions, decimals or percentages.

Note: while all numerical data is composed of numbers, not all numbers are numerical data. For example, postcodes, phone numbers and house numbers are all numbers but they are not numerical data.

It is important to be able to summarise numerical data so that it can be easily analysed and mathematical conclusions drawn from it. The following sections cover some important concepts in statistics.

Mean

The **mean** (or average) gives an idea of the centre point in a set of data. It is found by adding all the values in the data set together and then dividing the sum by the total number of values in the data set.

$$\textbf{\textit{mean}} = \frac{\textbf{\textit{sum of all values}}}{\textbf{\textit{number of values}}}$$

For example, if the data set is

$$2\ 4\ 3\ 9\ 11\ 13$$

the mean is $\frac{2+4+3+9+11+13}{6} = 7$.

Median

The **median** is the middle value of a data set once it is written in ascending order.

If there is an odd number of data elements, the median is the middle number. For example:

$$1\ 2\ 4\ \boxed{7}\ 9\ 13\ 17$$

If there is an even number of data elements, the median will be halfway between the two values in the middle (that is, the average of the two middle values). For example:

$$1\ 3\ 5\ 6\ 6\ \boxed{7\ 8}\ 9\ 9\ 11\ 12\ 24$$

$$\frac{7+8}{2} = 7.5$$

In this case, the median is not a value in the data set.

Mode

The **mode** is the value that occurs most frequently in a data set. For example, if the data set is

$$1\ 3\ 5\ 6\ 7\ 8\ \underline{9}\ \underline{9}\ 11\ 12\ 24$$

the mode is 9. It is the number that appears most often in the data set.

Sometimes a data set will have two modes. For example:

$$1\ 3\ 5\ \underline{6}\ \underline{6}\ 7\ 8\ \underline{9}\ \underline{9}\ 11\ 12\ 24$$

When there are two modes (6 and 9 in this example) the data set is called **bimodal**.

Range

The **range** is the difference between the smallest number and the largest number in a data set. For example, if the data set is

$$1\ 3\ 5\ 6\ 6\ 7\ 8\ 9\ 9\ 11\ 12\ 24$$

the range $= 24 - 1$

$= 23$.

Outlier

A value in a data set that is a long way away from the rest of the data is called an **outlier**. In the following example, all the data except one data element is 12 or less. The data element 24 is so far away from the rest of the data that it can be considered an outlier.

$$1\ 3\ 5\ 6\ 6\ 7\ 8\ 9\ 9\ 11\ 12\ \cancel{24}$$

Outliers often result from errors in counting or measuring and so they are removed from the data set. If they were kept, they could **skew** the data and give inaccurate values for the mean, mode, median and range.

Histograms

A common graph used to present numerical data is the **histogram**.

In a histogram the data is sorted into smaller ranges (called **class intervals**) and the number (or **frequency**) of data elements in each class interval is represented by a bar. The higher the bar, the greater the frequency. An example is shown below, along with instructions about how a histogram should be presented (with a title, labels on the axes etc.).

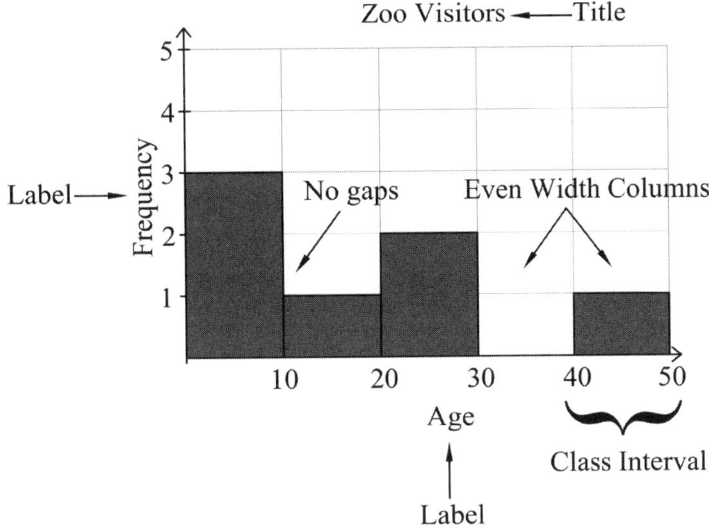

Example

The students in a Year 7 maths class were surveyed about how many pets they have. The results were

0 0 0 2 3 1 1 1 2 4 0 1 1 2 1 1 2 3 0 3

a. Determine the average number of pets owned by the students.

b. What was the most common number of pets owned?

c. Display the results in a histogram.

✓ *Solution*

Working	Explanation
a. $\frac{28}{20} = 1.4$	The average is also the mean, so use the formula for mean given earlier in this section (that is, find the sum of all the pets and divide the sum by the number of students in the survey).
b. The most common number of pets owned is 1.	Look for the value that occurs most frequently (that is, the mode).

c. 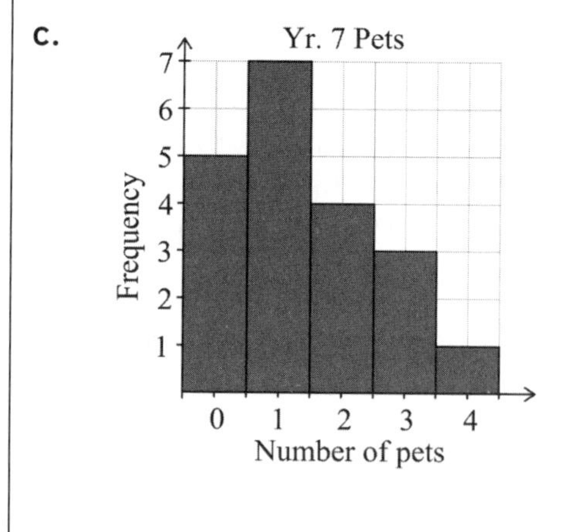	Checklist for creating a histogram: ✓ title ✓ labels on both axes ✓ columns of even width ✓ a scale on the frequency axis ✓ a scale on the horizontal axis ✓ no gaps between the columns **Note**: this example did not need to have the data sorted into class intervals.

Exercise 13.1

A group of school students were surveyed about their number of hours of screen time per day. The results were

3 5 10 9 3 6 7 4 8 3 2 2 4 10 2 5 6 2 4 7 8 9 4 6 2 1 5 5 5 6

a. Calculate the mean, median, mode and range of the data.

b. Display the data in a histogram with class intervals of 2 hours.

13.2 Dot plots and column graphs

In the last section we looked at numerical data: how it could be analysed and represented in a histogram. In this section we consider categorical data.

Categorical data is data that is grouped by category or type, not by number or class interval. Students' favourite colour, family car types and sport teams supported are all examples of categorical data.

A **dot plot** is a plot where each element in a data set is represented by a dot for the particular category to which it belongs. The example below is a dot plot representing the continents visited by a sample of 22 people.

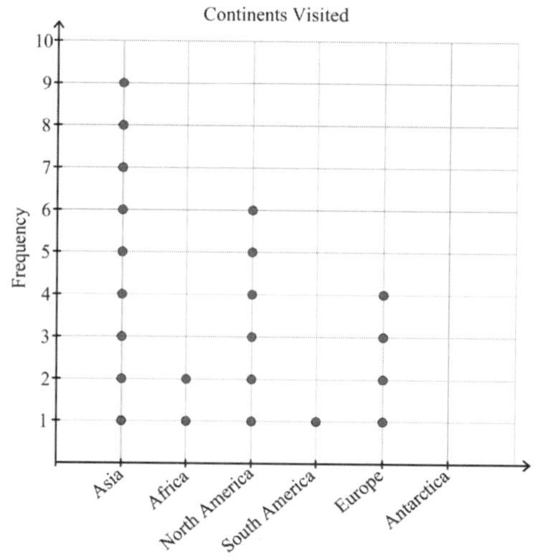

Note that the categories (in this example the continents) are listed along the horizontal axis and the frequency is represented on the vertical axis. Each person surveyed is represented by a dot. You can work out how many people in the sample visited a particular continent by counting the dots for that continent. (For example, two people visited Africa.)

A column graph is very similar to a dot plot. In a column graph the frequency of each category is represented by the height of a column. The higher the column, the greater the frequency. The column graph in the example below shows the favourite colours reported by a sample of students. You can see by the heights of the bars that yellow was the most popular favourite colour.

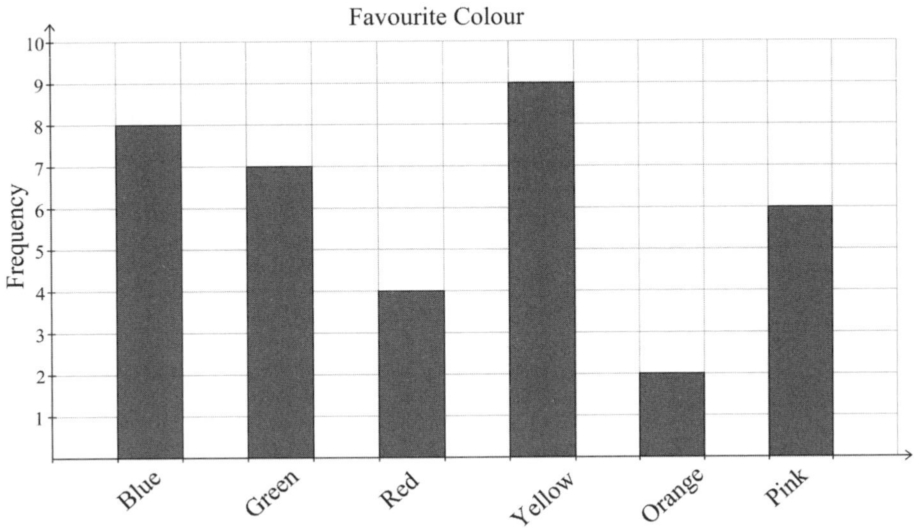

Both numerical data and categorical data can be displayed using a dot plot or column graph.

Example

The dot plot below shows the number of bedrooms in 20 apartments advertised online.

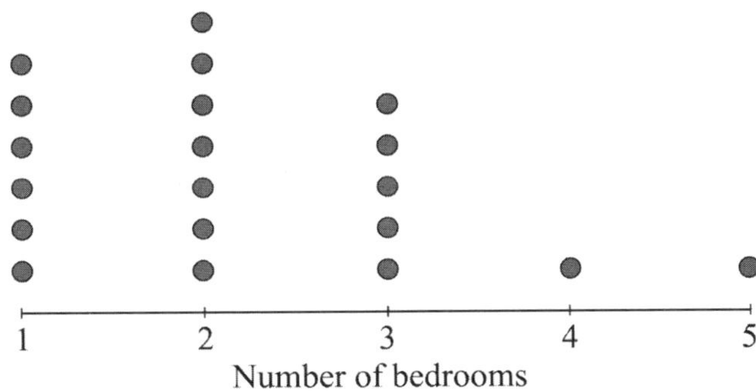

a. Calculate the mode of the data.

b. Calculate the median of the data.

✓ *Solution*

Working	Explanation
a. The most common number of bedrooms is 2.	The mode will be the value with the highest column (that is, the one with the most dots).
b. The median number of rooms is 2.	Since there are 20 apartments in this data (an even number), the median will be between the tenth and eleventh dots (that is, the average of the values represented by the tenth and eleventh dots). Start from the first dot at the bottom left and count up, then move to the bottom of the second column and count up, and so on. Both the tenth and eleventh dots represent a value of 2, and the average of two 2s is 2.

Exercise 13.2.1

The column graph below displays the results of a survey of a Year 7 class about sports played on weekends.

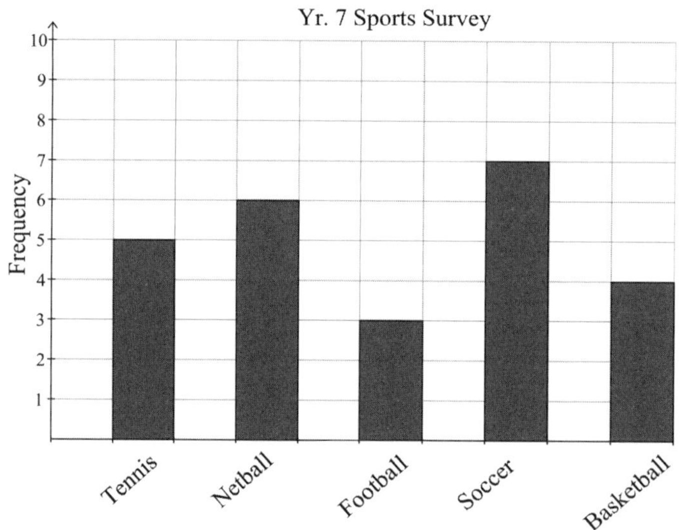

a. How many students were surveyed?

b. What is the most frequently played sport?

c. What percentage of students play tennis on weekends?

Exercise 13.2.2

The dot plot below shows how long, in minutes, it took 12 orders to be delivered from a restaurant.

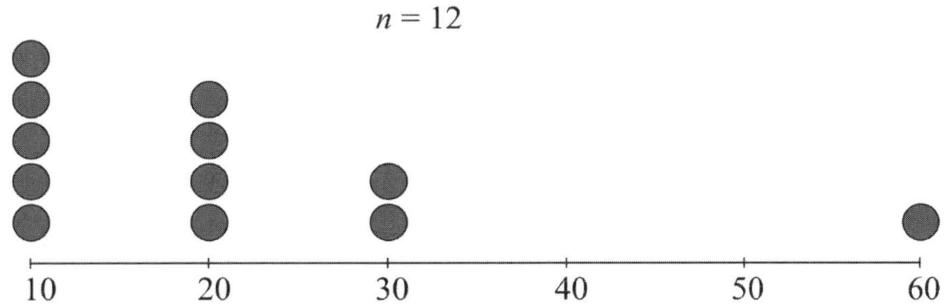

a. What is the median time of delivery?

b. Use a calculator to find the average time of delivery, to one decimal place.

c. What fraction of orders took 20 minutes?

d. If we remove the outlier, what are the new median and mean? Give your answer to one decimal place.

13.3 Line graphs

A **line graph** is a set of data points connected by straight line segments. Line graphs often show the relationship between a variable and time (that is, how the variable changes with respect to time).

Example

The line graph below shows the number of days that it rained in a city over a six-month period.

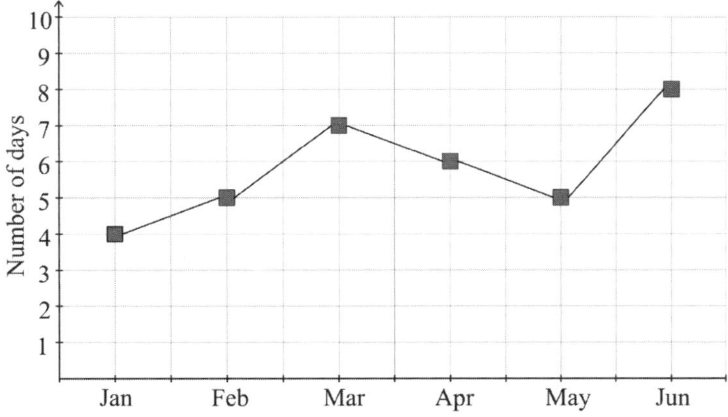

a. Which month had the most days of rain?

b. Which month had the highest number of days without rain?

c. What is the median number of days of rain over the six-month period?

d. What is the average number of days of rain for the period March to May?

✓ *Solution*

Working	Explanation
a. June had the highest number of rainy days.	The highest data point represents the month with the most rain. The scale on the vertical axis tells us that it rained 8 days in June.
b. January had the least number of rainy days: only 4.	The month with the highest number of days without rain is the month that has the least number of days with rain.
c. $4\ 5\ \underline{5\ 6}\ 7\ 8$ $\frac{5+6}{2} = 5.5$	To find the median number of rainy days, we must order the data from lowest to highest and then find the middle value.
d. $\frac{7+6+5}{3} = 6$	To find the average number of rainy days across the three months, add the values for each month together and then divide by 3.

Exercise 13.3.1

The line graph below shows the number of books read by a sample of students each month over a 12-month period.

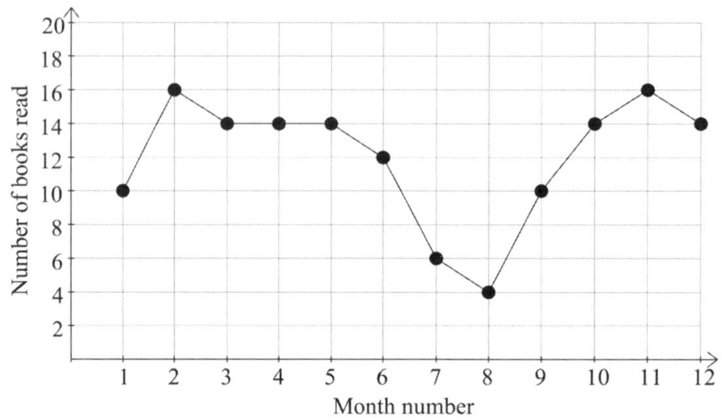

a. How many books were read in total over the 12 months?

b. In which month (or months) was the highest number of books read?

c. What is the average number of books read over the 12 months?

d. What is the median number of books read over the 12 months?

Exercise 13.3.2

The line graph below shows the height of an indoor plant, in centimetres, over an eight-year period.

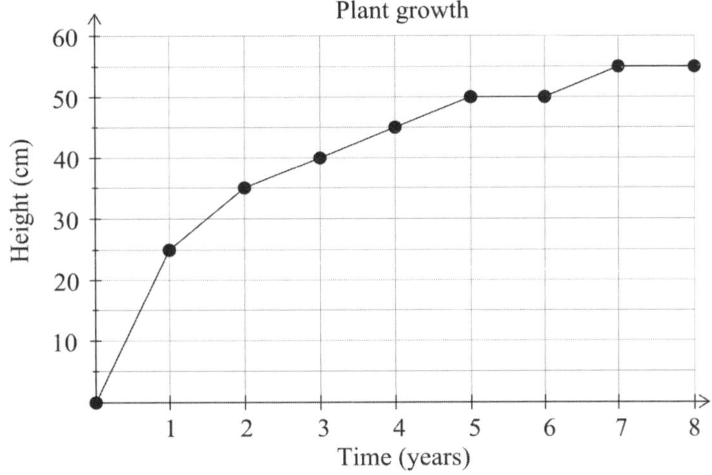

a. How tall was the plant after three years?

b. What happened between years 5 and 6?

c. During which period was the plant's growth most rapid?

d. In relation to the plant's height and age, what is the graph telling us?

13.4 Stem-and-leaf plots

When working with large amounts of data, a stem-and-leaf plot provides a simple way of viewing and organising the data. Patterns, averages, trends and outliers can all be easily seen from a stem-and-leaf plot. Two examples are shown below.

Stem: tens; leaf: units

stem	leaf
0	1 2 3 4 4
1	0 2 5 6
2	0 0 1 1 9

key $1|5 = 15$

Stem: hundreds/tens; leaf: units

stem	leaf
10	1 2 3 4 4
11	0 2 5 6
12	0 0 1 1 9

key $10|5 = 105$

The **stem** column is the first digit of a two-digit number (the tens), or the first two digits of a three-digit number (hundreds and tens).

The **leaf** column is the last digit of the value of a data element (the units).

The leaves are arranged in order, with the smallest closest to the stem and the largest furthest away from the stem.

You must always provide a **key** that explains how the stem and leaf combinations are to be interpreted. In the first example above, the key indicates that a 1 in the **stem** column and a 5 in the **leaf** column should be interpreted as 15. In the second example above, the key indicates that a 10 in the **stem** column and a 5 in the **leaf** column should be interpreted as 105.

Example

The following data are the results of test scores, as percentages, from a recent maths test.

75 78 66 52 80 95 88 75 75 82 55 92 60 88 70 86

a. Display the data in a stem-and-leaf plot.

b. How many students sat the test?

c. What is the median test score?

d. What is the most common test score?

✓ *Solution*

Working	Explanation
a. stem | leaf 5 | 2 5 6 | 0 6 7 | 0 5 5 5 8 8 | 0 2 6 8 8 9 | 2 5 key 7|5 = 75%	Make sure that the tens (in the stem column) are in ascending order vertically, and the ones (in the leaf columns) are in ascending order horizontally. It is important to add a key, especially when displaying percentages.
b. 16 students	To find the total number of students, count all the values in the leaf section.
c. $\frac{75 + 78}{2} = 76.5$ 76.5% is the median test score.	Given there are 16 data values (an even number), the median will be the average of the eighth and ninth values. Start counting from the first value in the first row of the leaf section.
d. 75% is the most common test score.	Look for the value that repeats itself most often.

Exercise 13.4.1

The following stem-and-leaf plot shows the percentage chance of rain per day forecast over the month of March.

stem	leaf
2	0 0 0 0
3	0 5 5 5
4	0 0 0 0 0 5
5	0 0 0 5 5
7	0 0 0 0 5
8	0 0

key $3|0 = 30\%$

a. What is the range of the data?

b. How many days were given more than a 60% chance of rain?

c. How many days were given less than a 35% chance of rain?

d. What is the median percentage chance of rain?

Exercise 13.4.2

The following stem-and-leaf plot shows the average daily temperature in different locations in Australia.

stem	leaf
1	5 6 7 8 8
2	0 2 3 4 4 5
3	0 1

key $1|7 = 17°\text{C}$

a. How many days were recorded in the data?

b. What are the minimum and maximum temperatures?

c. What is the range of the temperatures recorded?

d. What is the median temperature recorded?

13.5 Pie charts

Pie charts display groups of data as segments of a circle, with the size of each segment in direct proportion to the overall size of the data.

Example

The pie chart below shows the results of a survey of how a group of school students travel to school.

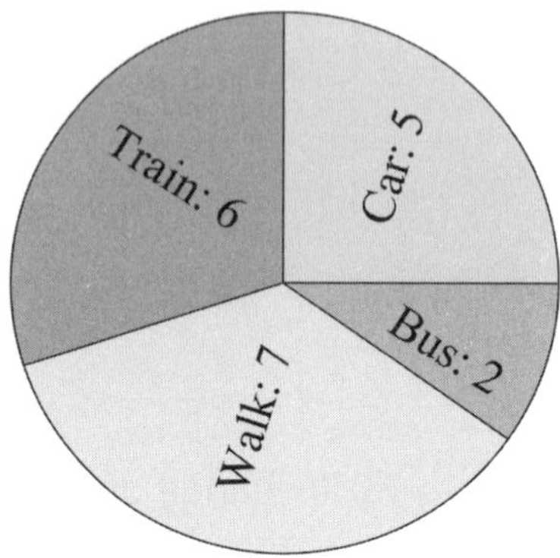

a. How many students were surveyed?

b. What was the most common response?

c. What fraction of students catch a bus to school?

d. What percentage of students ride to school in a car?

✓ *Solution*

Working	Explanation
a. 20	Count the numbers in each segment of the pie chart.
b. walk	From the pie chart we can see that walking to school was the most common response (7 out of 20).
c. $\frac{2}{20} = \frac{1}{10}$	From the pie chart we can see that 2 students out of 20 catch the bus to school. Always simplify fractions where possible.
d. $\frac{5}{20} \times 100 = 25\%$	From the pie chart we can see that 5 students out of 20 ride to school in a car.

Exercise 13.5

A survey of Year 7 students was conducted about which pets they have. The results were collated and represented in the following pie chart.

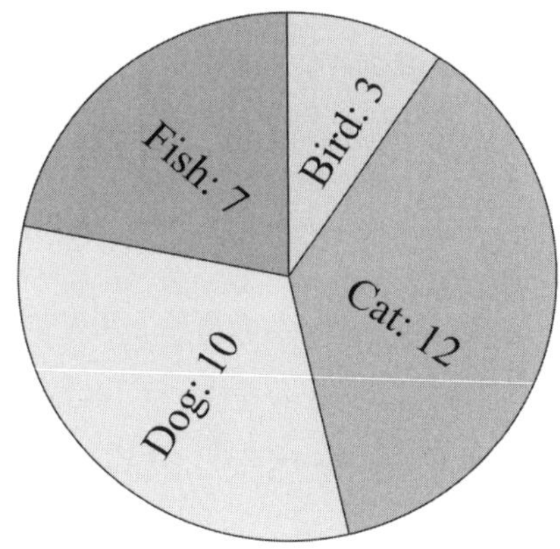

a. How many students were surveyed?

b. What was the most common response?

c. What fraction of students have a pet dog?

d. What percentage of students (correct to one decimal place) have a pet cat?

Answers

Exercise 13.1

a. mean = 5.1 hours, median = 5 hours, mode = 2 hours and 5 hours (bimodal), range = 9 hours

b.

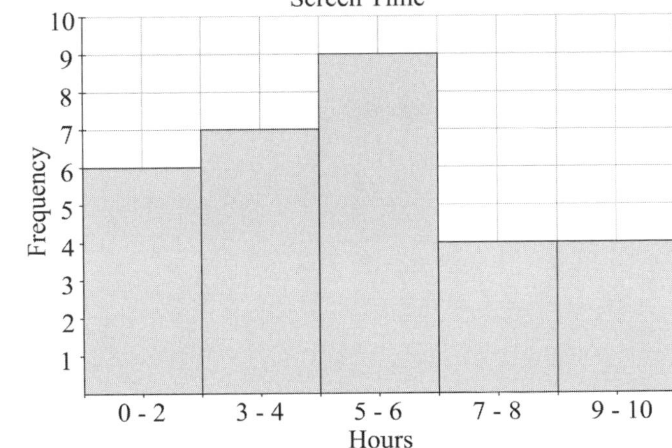

Exercise 13.2.1

a. 25

b. soccer

c. 20%

Exercise 13.2.2

a. 20 minutes

b. ≈ 20.8 minutes

c. $\frac{1}{3}$

d. median 20, mean ≈ 17.3

Exercise 13.3.1

a. 144
b. 2 and 11
c. 12
d. 14

Exercise 13.3.2

a. 40 cm
b. no growth
c. 0 to 1 year
d. The plant is reaching its maximum height.

Exercise 13.4.1

a. 60%
b. 7 days
c. 5 days
d. 42.5%

Exercise 13.4.2

a. 13 days
b. minimum 15°C, maximum 31°C
c. 16°C
d. 22°C

Exercise 13.5

a. 32 students
b. cat (12 students)
c. $\frac{5}{16}$
d. 37.5%

Chapter 14 – Probability

14.1 Introduction to probability

The chance or likelihood that something will occur is called its **probability**. For example, a coin has two sides, so the probability that it will land on heads when it is flipped into the air is 1 in 2 or $\frac{1}{2}$.

Probability is measured on a scale from 0 to 1, where 0 means that the occurrence of the event is impossible and 1 means that its occurrence is certain. The illustration below describes in words what various probability values or ranges mean.

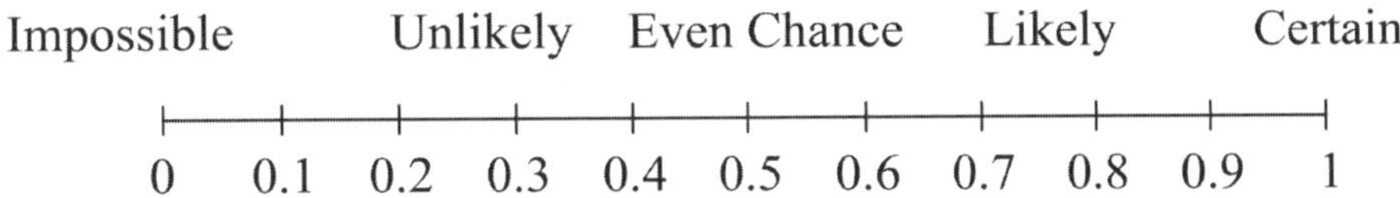

Probabilities can also be expressed as percentages or as fractions. The illustration below shows the same probabilities illustrated on the number line above as fractions.

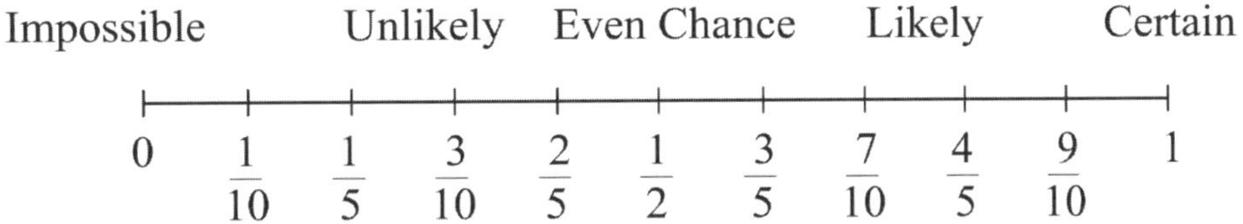

Example

Classify each of the following statements as true or false.

a. It is likely that a student in a Year 7 mathematics class will study probability at some time during the year.

b. There is an even chance that a flipped coin will land tails up.

c. Rolling a 1 on a six-sided die and flipping tails on a coin both have an even chance.

d. It is certain that a card drawn from a standard deck of 52 cards will be red or black.

✓ Solution

Working	Explanation
a. true	Probability is part of the Year 7 mathematics curriculum, so it is likely that schools will introduce it during the year.
b. true	Coins can only land heads or tails, and both outcomes are just as likely.
c. false	The chance of rolling a 1 is $\frac{1}{6}$ and the chance of flipping a tail is $\frac{1}{2}$.
d. true	With a normal deck (with no jokers), cards are either red or black.

Exercise 14.1.1

Classify each of the following statements as true or false.

a. An event is likely to happen if the probability is greater than 0.5.

b. An event is certain if its probability is 0.5.

c. Zero is not a possible probability.

d. Two is not a possible probability.

Exercise 14.1.2

For each of the following events, select the option below (**A–E**) that best describes the probability that it will occur.

A. impossible	B. unlikely	C. even chance	D. likely	E. certain

a. A card drawn from a standard deck of 52 cards will be the ace of clubs.

b. A card drawn from the same deck will be a heart.

c. A card drawn from the same deck will be black.

d. The sun will rise tomorrow.

e. A flipped coin will land tails up.

f. A person selected at random will be left-handed.

14.2 Theoretical probability

Theoretical probability is the probability of an **event** occurring based on how many possible outcomes there are.

An event could be a single **outcome**, such as rolling a 5 with a six-sided die. Or it could be a number of possible outcomes, such as rolling an even number. (In the second case there are three possible outcomes: 2, 4 and 6.)

The set of all possible outcomes is called the **sample space**.

The theoretical probability of an event occurring is calculated by the following formula.

$$\textit{probability} = \frac{\textit{number of outcomes where the event could occur}}{\textit{total number of possible outcomes}}$$

Example

A standard six-sided die is rolled.

a. Write down the sample space.

b. Calculate the probability of rolling a 2.

c. Calculate the probability of rolling an even number.

d. Calculate the probability of rolling a number less than 5.

✓ ***Solution***

Working	Explanation
a. $S = \{1, 2, 3, 4, 5, 6\}$	The sample space, S, is the set of all possible outcomes. Use set notation: $\{\}$.
b. $\Pr(2) = \frac{1}{6}$	We write $\Pr(2)$ as shorthand for 'the probability that the outcome is 2'. A die has six faces and each face has a different number. The number 2 is one outcome out of six possible outcomes.
c. $\Pr(\text{even}) = \frac{3}{6}$ $= \frac{1}{2}$	There are three even numbers in the sample space, so there are three possible outcomes in the event of rolling an even number. Therefore the possibility of the event is three out of a total of six possible outcomes. Simplify the fraction.
d. $\Pr(n < 5) = \frac{4}{6}$ $= \frac{2}{3}$	There are four values less than 5 in the sample space, so there are four possible outcomes in the event of rolling a number less than 5. Therefore the possibility of the event is four out of a total of six possible outcomes. Simplify the fraction. **Note:** $\Pr(\text{less than } 5)$ is also an acceptable notation for the probability of an event.

Exercise 14.2.1

A letter is chosen at random from the word MATHEMATICS. Determine each of the following probabilities as a fraction expressed in its simplest form.

a. The probability that the letter is E.

b. The probability that the letter is M.

c. The probability that the letter is T or S.

Exercise 14.2.2

Consider the following spinner.

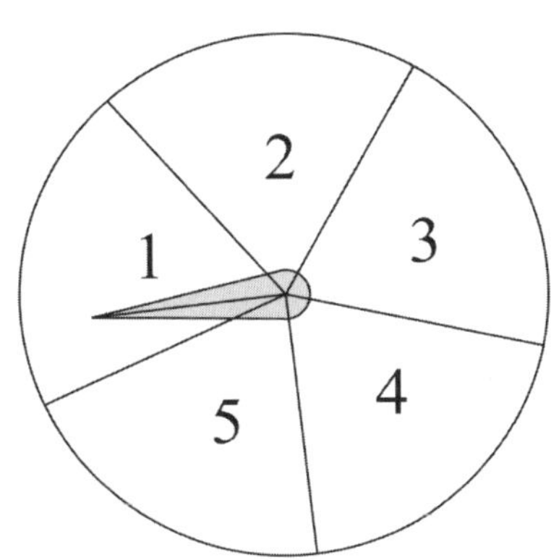

Determine the probability of

a. spinning a 3

b. spinning an even number

c. spinning a number greater than 2

d. spinning a factor of 4

e. spinning a perfect square.

14.3 Experimental probability

Theoretical probability is what the probability **should** be based on how many possible outcomes there are. **Experimental probability** is the probability based on what **did** happen in a random experiment.

A **random experiment** is one that can be repeated under the same conditions. Each repetition in a random experiment is called a **trial**. For example, if we were running an experiment to see if a coin is a fair coin (and so has an equal chance of landing heads or tails when flipped), a single flip of the coin is a trial.

Example

A spinner with the numbers 1, 2, 3 and 4 on it is spun 20 times and the following numbers came up.

$$4, 3, 2, 3, 1, 1, 1, 3, 2, 4, 4, 2, 2, 1, 3, 2, 1, 1, 4, 1$$

a. What is the experimental probability of getting a 1?

b. What is the experimental probability of getting an even number?

c. Compare your answer from part **b.** to the theoretical probability of this event occurring.

d. Based on this experiment, how many 3s would you expect to get if you spun the spinner 100 times?

✓ *Solution*

Working	Explanation
a. $\frac{7}{20}$	The number 1 came up seven times out of a total of 20 spins.
b. $\frac{9}{20}$	The numbers 2 and 4 came up nine times out of a total of 20 spins.
c. The theoretical probability of an even number is $\frac{1}{2}$ but the experimental probability is $\frac{9}{20}$.	When comparing theoretical to experimental probabilities, we need both probabilities to be in fractions or both in decimals.
d. $\frac{4}{20} \times 100 = 20$	The number 3 came up four times. To find the expected probability, multiply the experimental probability by the number of trials.

Exercise 14.3.1

A standard six-sided die was rolled 20 times and the following results were recorded.

$$1, 6, 4, 2, 1, 4, 3, 2, 2, 5, 6, 1, 2, 4, 2, 4, 1, 4, 6, 3$$

a. What is the experimental probability of rolling a 3?

b. What is the experimental probability of rolling a number greater than 4?

c. Based on this experiment, how many even numbers would you expect to see if you rolled the die 1000 times?

Exercise 14.3.2

A spinner has three unequal segments, coloured yellow, blue and red. The table below shows the results of spinning the spinner 40 times.

Colour	Frequency
Yellow	16
Blue	10
Red	14

a. Based on this experiment what is the probability of spinning yellow?

b. What is the probability of spinning a colour other than blue?

c. How many times would you expect to spin red in 1000 spins?

Answers

Exercise 14.1.1

a. true b. false c. false d. true

Exercise 14.1.2

a. B b. B c. C d. E e. C f. B

Exercise 14.2.1

a. $\frac{1}{11}$ b. $\frac{2}{11}$ c. $\frac{3}{11}$

Exercise 14.2.2

a. $\frac{1}{5}$ b. $\frac{2}{5}$ c. $\frac{3}{5}$ d. $\frac{3}{5}$ e. $\frac{2}{5}$

Exercise 14.3.1

a. $\frac{1}{10}$ b. $\frac{1}{5}$ c. 650

Exercise 14.3.2

a. $\frac{2}{5}$ b. $\frac{3}{4}$ c. 350

Chapter 15 – Algorithms

An **algorithm** is a process or set of rules that can be followed to solve a problem or make a decision.

There are many different examples of algorithms, and the following is one example. Suppose we have a diagram where two lines are crossed by another line. An algorithm to determine whether two angles in the diagram are co-interior is given below.

Step 1. Are both angles inside the two lines that are crossed?

If YES, go to Step 2.

If NO, write 'The angles are not co-interior.'

Step 2. Are both angles on the same side of the line that crosses the other lines?

If YES, go to Step 3.

If NO, write 'The angles are not co-interior.'

Step 3. Is the sum of the angles equal to $180°$?

If YES, write 'The angles are co-interior.'

If NO, write 'The angles are not co-interior.'

Example

Use the algorithm above to determine if the angles below are co-interior.

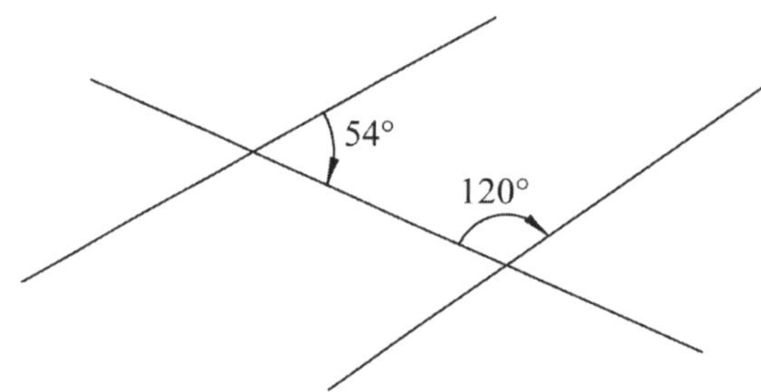

✓ *Solution*

Working	Explanation
Both angles are inside two lines that are crossed by a transversal line.	**Step 1:** Are both angles inside two lines that are crossed by a transversal line? Follow the YES instruction.
Both angles are on the same side of the transversal line.	**Step 2:** Are both angles on the same side of the line that crosses the other lines? Follow the YES instruction.
$54 + 120 \neq 180$	**Step 3:** Do the angles sum to $180°$? No: the angles are not co-interior.

Exercise 15.1

Use the algorithm to determine whether the angles in the following diagrams are co-interior.

a.

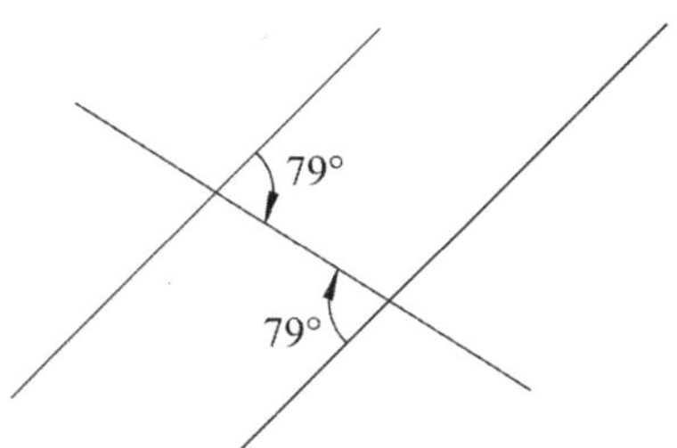

b.

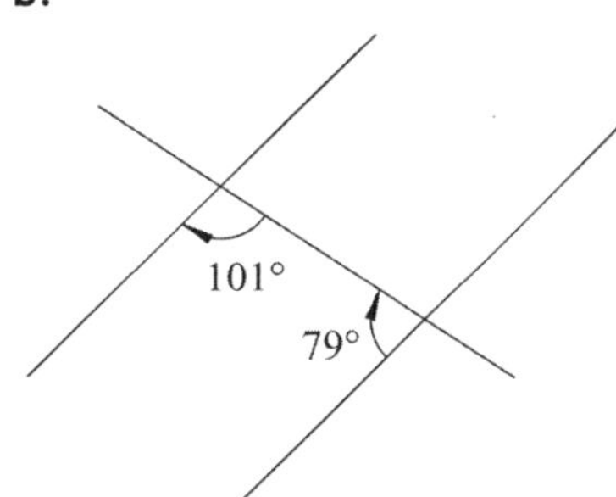

c.

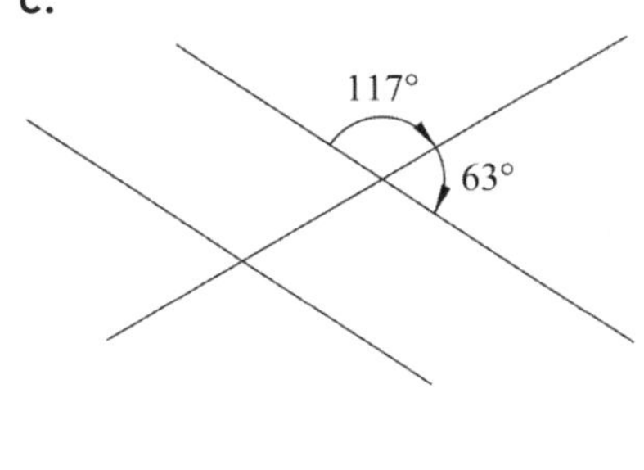

Answers

Exercise 15.1

- **a.** No, as the angles are not on the same side of the transversal line.
- **b.** Yes, the angles are co-interior.
- **c.** No, as the angles are not inside the lines that are crossed by the transversal line.